# The Collector's Encyclopedia of
# BRUSH-McCOY POTTERY

## UPDATED VALUES

## Sharon & Bob Huxford

## COLLECTOR BOOKS
*A Division of Schroeder Publishing Co., Inc.*

The current values in this book should be used only as a guide. They are not intended to set prices, which vary from one section of the country to another. Auction prices as well as dealer prices vary greatly and are affected by condition as well as demand. Neither the Authors nor the Publisher assumes responsibility for any losses that might be incurred as a result of consulting this guide.

*Searching For A Publisher?*

We are always looking for knowledgeable people considered to be experts within their fields. If you feel that there is a real need for a book on your collectible subject and have a large comprehensive collection, contact Collector Books.

# CONTENTS

# DEDICATION

To Lucile whose loving memories of her
father caused this book to be written.

*Mr. and Mrs. W. Clare Barnett*

# ACKNOWLEDGMENTS

This book was first published in 1978, when interest in pottery collecting was just beginning to take hold. Roseville, Weller, and Rookwood collectors were already solidly entrenched, but they were attracted for the most part to the fine art ware lines produced during the early years of those Ohio institutions. Cookie jars — especially McCoy's — had been collectible for a few years, but in general, there was little enthusiasm for the other wares of either the McCoy or the Brush potteries. Part of this indifference was due to the simple fact that at that time we had no idea as to what kind of wares either pottery had made during their years of productivity. As McCoy's extensive line of cookie jars began to draw attention to their novelty planters and vases, a collector cult began to develop whose only requirement of the pottery they hunted for was that it be marked McCoy. So in 1975, we published our book *The Collector's Encyclopedia of McCoy Pottery*.

The friendly rivalry of the Brush and McCoy families was still a little bit evident even at that point in time, and while we were still in Zanesville doing our research and taking photographs for the McCoy book, we met Lucile Brush Barnett, daughter of George Brush, the founder of the original Brush pottery. Lucile had grown up during the prolific years of her father's company, and she not only had original catalogs and extensive documentation in her possession but also was able to recall personal experiences and observations as though they had taken place yesterday, not fifty years prior. She came to us bent on a mission. Motivated by love for her father and wanting to preserve the history of his company, she presented to us the notion that we should also do a Brush book. The old factory still stood, and packed away in its storeroom was more than enough lovely pottery to represent each phase of production — art ware, kitchen ware, novelty items, and cookie jars. We couldn't say no to her. In the first place, with her help the book would practically write itself, and secondly, it would have been very difficult to disappoint Lucile. We soon fell in love with this warm-hearted lady with the beautiful brown eyes. Her husband, Clare, a Zanesville native, had worked in the pottery since 1928 when he was a young man of 22, eventually becoming president and general manager. Work soon began on the book, and Clare was able to add to Lucile's outline with information on lines he had designed, glazes he had developed, the working of the machinery, and casting and firing techniques.

The book was quickly completed and when it was released, it sent shock waves throughout the network of pottery collectors around the country. Pieces once believed to be Roseville or Weller were finally correctly identified. Catalog reprints showed blue and white stoneware as well as a line of yellow ware with the Rockingham glaze. But we always have felt that this book was really ahead of its time. After the original printing was gone, there seemed to be very little demand for the book, and Collector Books decided not to reprint. Recently, though, Brush pottery seems to have come into its own, and so through popular request, we again offer *The Collector's Encyclopedia of Brush-McCoy Pottery*. We hope you enjoy reading it now, nearly twenty years after we did our original research and photography. We still remember the thrill of pulling into the parking lot there in front of the old Brush Pottery and stepping back in time. To pottery lovers and especially to pottery editors, an experience like we had inside that old building is one we could never put a price on. What a treat! Thank you, Lucile and Clare, for giving us that special memory.

There were many people who assisted us as we worked on the original book. Their help is no less appreciated today than it was all those years ago. So we would like to repeat our original lists of Acknowledgements, though some of these people have since passed away and relationships may have changed.

This is a section we look forward to writing — when we have an opportunity to publicly express our personal gratitude to the many wonderful people who have contributed to virtually every phase of this book — yet no feeling is harder to convey articulately! To merely say "thank you" seems so inadequate! But please know how very, very much we do appreciate each and every one of you who in any way helped to make *The Collector's Encyclopedia of Brush-McCoy* a realization.

We're so pleased to be able to offer our readers a history so complete. To a great extent the credit for this goes to Mrs. Lucile Brush Barnett — and for her this has been a labor of love. She is a lady of amazing energy, a clear mind with fascinating recall, and twinkling dark brown eyes that match those in her father's photographs. And through Mr. Barnett's recollections we could glimpse the past and better understand the procedures and techniques that were used in the manufacture of the pottery. We so very much enjoyed the time we spent with you both; thank you for your help, and for the many personal kindnesses you showed us while we were in Zanesville.

There are three men who deserve special recognition:

Norris Schneider has written many articles and books which have stimulated interest in Ohio pottery. He kindly provided us with information pertinent to the history of the first Brush Pottery — and for this as well as for the facts gleaned from his past writings, we are sincerely grateful.

Jay Cusick provided the photograph of his father, A. L. Cusick, and outlined his career in the industry for us. He loaned several outstanding pieces of fine old pottery and helped tremendously in many other ways.

"Wib" Smith located many pieces of the pottery at flea markets and antique stores and searched through obscure corners of the factory to find any long-forgotten ware we might need to photograph. "Wib" was also able to contribute information concerning some of the older employees.

These people loaned pottery from their collections — and without their generosity some of the lines could not have been properly represented: Maxene Ferguson, Wayside Antiques; Mrs. Nelson McCoy; Madeleine Downey Zollar; Harold Nichols; Connie and Mike Nickel; Pauline and Wade Prentis; Mildred Bowen; Russel "Russ" McNeal; Mrs. Carl Sagle; Moses Mesre; and Mrs. Earl Cavinee.

Those who helped with the research and contributed essential information are: James R. Marsh, Asst. Secretary of the State of Ohio; Mrs. George Dunzweiler; Atty. John Ringhisen; John Tatman; and Mrs. Helen Jamieson Longstreth.

There were others who helped in various ways — Linda Willett; Cy Lambert; Betty Blair; Bill Barnett; Dr. Charles Dietz of the Art Center and his staff; Sally Zinnsmeester; Joan Leasure; Harold Hays; and Sam Allen.

As always, Mom and Dad, Mr. and Mrs. Ray Newnum, and Bob's mother, Ruth Huxford, held things together for us at home while we were on the road.

Our photographer was Ted Wright — and he did a beautiful job.

To all of you — and to anyone whose name we inadvertently omitted — your enthusiasm, your encouragement, and your assistance is appreciated very, very much. God bless you all.

Because our own interests have changed over the past twenty years, we are no longer personally involved in collecting Brush-McCoy pottery. So we're grateful to Margaret and Robert Hanson and their son Harper for their assistance in compiling current pricing information. The photographs we have added for this edition are from the Hanson collection.

# FOREWORD

The office building still stands on Dearborn Street in Zanesville, Ohio — today looking much different than it did during the years when the clay industry was at its zenith. The fire in 1918 destroyed the manufacturing portion that had been added to the old J. B. Owens building when it was purchased in 1911. And now the old edifice recalls the original construction — the lettering is faded, of course, but still one can easily read "J. B. Owens, Plant No. 1" in white block characters against now-worn bricks no doubt locally burned from the red Ohio clays. The windows are covered with corrugated green fiberglass panels — necessary precautions speaking a sad commentary on the crimes of this era. In the crushed rock of the parking lot one may find tiny unglazed white ceramic floor tile — the Owen's tile company was just next door, years ago.

The train tracks that used to carry off car loads of pottery with "not a sleeper or sticker in the lot" (if the promise of the old 1916 catalog was accurate) remains, still in use.

Inside the building are mementos of the early years. The offices remain much the same now as then — and upstairs in the corner of the room now used only for storage, rests an old dust-covered trunk — one that salesmen carried their samples in when they would rent hotel rooms to display their merchandise as they traveled from city to city. On the side of the trunk are the stenciled letters: "The J. W. McCoy Pottery Co." Down in the vault is the safe, transferred to the J. W. McCoy Pottery Company with the purchase of the building; nevertheless, it still remains as it was when it was new — it must have been a source of pride to the original owner, its black surface enlivened with the work of some now-unknown artist, and over the door, the words: "J. B. Owens Pottery Co." Inside, saved through the years though faded from a crisp white to a mellow parchment, are photographs, records, and catalogs that reveal the whole picture of the birth and growth of a pottery — colorful with well-remembered names: J. W. McCoy, John B. Owens, George S. Brush, A. L. Cusick, A. Radford, Watt Pottery, Mosaic Tile — all mingling and interwoven, one with the other, at one time and then another.

# HISTORY AND DEVELOPMENT OF THE BRUSH-McCOY POTTERY

The pottery that later became The Brush Pottery had roots in many beginnings, evolved from many mergers.

Its earlist forerunner was the J. W. McCoy Pottery Company, named after the founder and first president. Though located in Roseville, Perry County, Ohio, the firm was incorporated in West Virginia to take advantage of that state's lower taxation rate. The firm continued to do business in Ohio as a foreign corporation until July 1905, when the original charter was dissolved.

PAGE .....................

PLEASE RETURN WITH YOUR REMITTANCE.

*Charleston, W. Va., Sept 5, 1899*

*The J.W. McCoy Pottery Co,*

*Roseville, Ohio,*

To **Wm. M. O. Dawson**, Secretary of State, Dr.

REMIT BY CERTIFIED CHECK, MONEY ORDER, OR BANK DRAFT

| | | |
|---|---|---|
| To issuing Certificate of Incorporation to *The J. W. McCoy Pottery Co,* | 6 | 00 |
| To Certified Copy of same and Tax on State Seal, | 5 | 00 |
| To Annual License Tax on Corporation to May first, next, | 50 | 00 |
| | | |
| Total, - - - - - - - $ | 61 | 00 |

Received payment, *Sept 5*, 1899.

*Wm M O Dawson* Secretary of State.

By ............................., Chief Clerk.

77 25

8

*Company letterhead in use around 1901 – 1904*

The original capital of $15,200 had substantially increased to $100,000 by October 1, 1901. Officers and stockholders are indicated on the above letterhead. In addition to those listed, D. Zinnsmeester also served for a time on the board of directors.

The earliest ware manufactured by the company consisted of kitchenwares such as bowls and bake pans, crocks and kettles as well as the blended glazed majolica-type cupsidors, jardinieres, pedestals, and umbrella stands that were so popular in the early 1900s. But also during the few years the company was in operation before the fire of 1903, they attempted to produce at least two lines of art pottery. The first line, called Mt. Pelee, was introduced around 1902. Many authorities believe it was inspired by ancient pottery found in the ruins of St. Pierre on the Isle of Martinique about this time. Probably much of this ware was destroyed in the fire, and there are no records to indicate further attempts to produce it. Although any piece marked Mt. Pelee is very rare, of the two types of glazes known to exist, the one more likely to be found is an iridescent charcoal gray — the second type is a mat green glaze. Although a molded line, the appearance of the ware indicates that while the clay body was still wet and pliable, it was pulled and pinched with the fingers to form sharp crests and peaks — this is the identifying characteristic common to the line. When handles were used, they were applied, never smooth or symmetrical, but rather twisted and knarled — the style very eccentric.

In April 1903, a devastating fire swept through the building, destroying the kiln shed, warehouse, packing departments, and the entire stock of pottery. By the end of the year, however, repairs and rebuilding had progressed far enough to allow production to resume. (From *Art Pottery of the United States*, by Paul Evans.)

The catalog from 1904 shows illustrations of another artistic line called Rosewood. Twelve vase shapes and two large jardinieres were offered in the standard brown glaze, decorated only with diagonal streaks of contrasting bright orange. Prices were approximately double those of the blended lines, with a large jardiniere listed at $48 per dozen.

When the new facilities were completed on Perry Street in Roseville early in 1905, the stockholders voted unanimously to become an Ohio corporation. A page from the old record book reveals this purpose: "We the undersigned, all of whom are citizens of the state of Ohio, desiring to form a corporation for profit under the general corporation laws of said state, do hereby certify . . . (that) said corporation is formed for the purpose of manufacturing glazed and unglazed pottery, tile, brick, and terra cotta ware and dealing and trafficking in the same . . . the capital stock of said corporation shall be One Hundred Twenty-Five Thousand Dollars ($125,000.00) divided into Twelve hundred fifty (1250) shares of One hundred Dollars ($100.00) each. In Witness Whereof, we have here unto set our hands, this 27th day of January, A.D., 1905." James W. McCoy, F. M. Rider, G. W. Walker, W. R. Baker, George H. Stewart and C. Stolzenbach. (Although Stolzenbach retained his position as president of the company through the early months of 1905, the certificate that dissolved the foreign corporation issued by the state of West Virginia in July of that year names William H. Baker as president of the company. Mr. Baker served in that capacity until his death in December 1932.)

In 1906, McCoy's brother-in-law, D. L. Melick was hired as secretary; a second brother-in-law, Mr. Landon, worked part-time selling stock.

Several new art lines were introduced during the next few years, and although perhaps falling behind some of the highly competitive potteries in the number of such lines in production, the J. W. McCoy Pottery Company nevertheless developed some very fine art pottery. The first art ware to be produced in their new facilities was called Loy-Nel-Art — a standard brown ware with underglaze slip decoration. It was named after J. W. McCoy's three sons, Lloyd, Nelson, and Arthur. Floral subjects were the most popular; it is very unusual to find another type. Very rarely did the artists sign their work. Only two signed examples have been reported, one signed Chilcote, and the other T. S. Although not always marked, some pieces carry in die-impressed letters: Loy-Nel-Art, McCoy.

Two other lines of exceptional quality were also produced after 1905. Both are characterized by a cameo-type decoration, molded into the ware, usually simple floral studies or leaves and berries done predominantly in shades of soft beige to orange on a beautiful high gloss brown glaze. Either line may be further decorated with the diagonal orange streaks introduced with the 1904 Rosewood line. No obvious differences can be cited between the lines, although some pieces of this type are marked in incised lettering "Olympia, McCoy" or "Rosewood, McCoy" (to which we would add: Second Line).

A very rare example of another art line no doubt produced during this period is decorated with a flowing Art Nouveau-style poppy, executed in very heavy slip painting on brown glaze. It is signed "Chilcote" and marked "Renaissance, McCoy."

In 1908, the man who was to be the company's principal designer for many years became associated with the J. W. McCoy Pottery Company. His name was Albert Logan Cusick, and his talents had already earned him recognition in the field of art pottery.

George S. Brush became a stockholder of the J. W. McCoy Pottery, according to the minutes of the January 14, 1909, meeting, and was immediately elected secretary and general manager. (J. W. McCoy was elected to the office of vice president at the same meeting.) George Brush first became involved in the pottery industry in 1901 when he accepted a position with the J. B. Owens Pottery Company in Zanesville. Undoubtedly Brush never dreamed that this involvement would ultimately lead to his being the president of his own pottery on those very premises. But before this would occur, there would be many changes and developments that would lead to that destination.

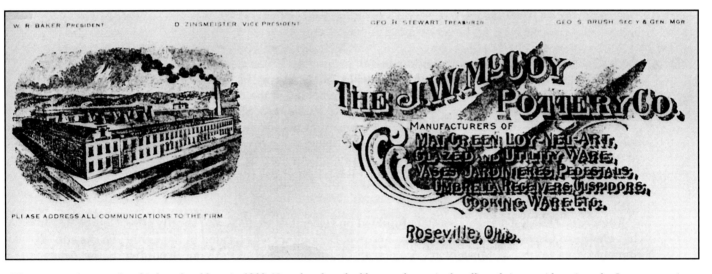

*The company began using this letterhead later in 1909. Note that there had been a change in the office of vice president since the January meeting.*

11

John B. Owens moved to Zanesville, Ohio, in 1891, a move no doubt prompted by an offer of a free tract of land for a factory site from the Spangler Realtors of Brighton — if he would move his factory from Roseville. But J. B. Owens did these speculators one step better; he shrewdly demanded $5,000.00 for the honor of his presence in Zanesville (but of necessity compromised on $4,500.00! This may have been the parcel of land deeded to the J. B. Owens Pottery Company on December 30, 1892, by J. B. Owens for the sum of $1.00 as recorded in the Records of Deeds in the Muskingum County Courthouse. A second transaction also noted was the purchase of the land from David H. Harris for the sum of $2,500.00, in the Brighton section of the city, where Owens constructed his pottery). The J. B. Owens Pottery Company was incorporated on September 24, 1891, and by December 15 of that year the first kiln had been burned. He continued to make stoneware of the type he had previously produced in Roseville until 1896 when he began the manufacture of fine art pottery.

The position George Brush accepted with Owens in 1901 was as the head of their printing department. He was quite experienced in the printers' trade, since he had worked for daily newspapers and job-printing offices since the age of fifteen. The 1904 catalog he printed for Owens consisted of forty pages measuring 14" x 20", and contained eight hundred pieces of ware. For almost five years Brush was in charge of reporting, editing, printing, and publishing *The Owens Monthly*. When this publication was discontinued in 1905, he continued with the Owens company as secretary and sales manager until 1907.

On October 16, 1905, Owens reorganized, and formed a corporation known as the Zanesville Tile Company. After April 30, 1906, the production of art pottery was stopped, and tile was produced exclusively. (The property was deeded to the Zanesville Tile Company in 1906, and the J. B. Owens Pottery Company was dissolved on April 19, 1907.) Owens remained at the original location until the company closed in October 1909, when he sold this property to William M. Shinnick — thereafter this tract was often referred to as the Wm. Shinnick land. Owens built his second pottery directly across the street, where he continued to manufacture floor and wall tile until the building burned in 1930, according to the Zanesville Fire Department records. Although no further tile was manufactured, the date recorded with the State of Ohio indicating the dissolution of the company was November 16, 1936, two years after Owens' death.

The Brush Pottery Company was incorporated on December 10, 1906, and soon thereafter, George Brush left Owens to begin to produce pottery on his own. His pottery was located in Zanesville, on the site of the old Union Pottery at Muskingum Avenue and Jefferson Street in Putnam. According to the Zanesville City Directory, 1907, the officers of the company were: W. C. Mooney, President; W. B. Cosgrave, Vice President; G. S. Brush, Secretary and Treasurer; A. C. Tatman, Superintendent. Their original capital was $25,000. Early in December 1907, they began work — producing sanitary Bristol ware, kitchen and toilet specialties, mugs and oyster bowls. On January 10, 1908, they were commissioned to make Bear banks, Bear pitchers, saggers, and salt box lids. Evidence would support the theory that the Lucile Line (named for Brush's daughter Lucile who was born in 1906) originated at this first Brush Pottery, for in their old payroll book piecework is noted for a line referred to as "Luc" — which is exactly how this line was indicated in later Brush-McCoy records. After being in production just a few days less than one year, the Brush Pottery burned — but the tragedy was soon revealed to be a blessing in disguise, when within only a short time the area was completely flooded. Although Brush's fire loss was only partially covered in insurance, he had carried none for flooding!

*Remains of the Brush Pottery after the fire of 1908.*

The following vivid account of that fire is taken from the Zanesville and Muskingum County Ohio History by Thomas Lewis, Vol. II, page 555:

The year was closing when fire destroyed the Brush Pottery Company's plant on Muskingum Avenue, located in the building which had been built by the Buckinghams in 1853 for the manufacture of buckets, but which became a planing mill operated by Guthrie and Taylor. The flames, of unknown origin, were seen soon after mid-night on November 26 (1908). A gallant fight was made to save it, but this failed. Surrounding property, however, was kept from destruction.

Danger from falling walls hampered the firemens' efforts from mid-night on. By day-break, building, machinery, stocks, etc., were gone — of the first, only black and ragged walls remaining. A great throng had watched the work of destruction.

The Curtis lumber yards and office were near at hand. The lumber at least, was in imminent danger from flying sparks and would have been consumed had it not been dampened by the rain which had fallen. The heat was so intense that it drove the firemen back again and again. Pluck and duty sent them back until streams of water were attacking the flames from all sides. Bystanders broke into the office and rescued books and valuable papers.*

The structure was a two-story brick with stone foundation. The loss was about $20,000 partly covered by insurance.

*(These papers included the payroll book from the founding in December 1907, and probably some catalog sheets.)

Soon after the fire in 1908, Brush leased the Crooksville Clay Products Company, where he stored pottery, molds, saggers, etc., which he had been able to salvage. He became manager of the Globe Stoneware Company and sold his wares, the Lucile Toilet Ware among them, through a catalog carrying the company name, Zanesville-Crooksville Sales Company.

The Brush Pottery continued to exist as a corporation until 1912, even though George Brush had joined the McCoy firm in 1909, and on August 24, 1911, Brush purchased the Wm. Shinnick property (formerly J. B. Owens Plant No. 1) on Dearborn Street. In deference to the J. B. Owens Floor and Wall Tile Company which was located nearby, restrictions were placed on the building — no floor, wall, or fireplace tile was to be made, sold, or stored there. (It is interesting to note that in the minutes of the meeting of the board on October 12, 1917, it was reported by George Brush that he had inspected a continuous kiln in operation at the J. B. Owens plant in Metuchen, New Jersey.)

The October 23, 1911, minutes of the directors' meeting of the J. W. McCoy Pottery Company indicated the purchase of the Globe Stoneware Company. Further business discussed at that meeting was an offer by George Brush to sell them the "molds, saggers, catalogs and real estate known as the Wm. Shinnick land." On November 7, 1911, the directors voted to accept Brush's offer to sell and called for a stockholders meeting on December 13 to consider the propriety of changing the company name. The vote taken at that meeting was unanimous, J. W. McCoy concurring, to change the name of the pottery to "The Brush-McCoy Pottery Company."

The Brush-McCoy Pottery Company reorganized, the capital was increased to $200,000, and these new officers were elected: W. R. Baker, President; T. L. Moorhead, Vice President; S. M. Seright, Secretary; George H. Stewart, Treasurer; and George Brush, General Manager. Wm. Bateman was elected to succeed J. W. McCoy on the Board of Directors. If indeed McCoy's interest would seem to wane at this point, it can most likely be attributed to the fact that in 1910, he and his son Nelson founded the Nelson McCoy Sanitary Stoneware Company in Roseville, Ohio. Aside from this, he lived only three years longer, and quite possibly his health was failing.

The offices of the pottery moved to the Zanesville plant, which was designated Plant No. 1, the Roseville location being Plant No. 2. Both locations were improved and enlarged, new round kilns were added to total nineteen in both plants. According to the Zanesville *Daily Courier*, December 14, 1911, the company was "in a position to compete with the largest pottery manufacturers both as to capacity and working capital. The output will consist of art and utility ware, stoneware and cooking ware" with artware to be made at Zanesville, and the stoneware and cooking ware at the Roseville location.

Some of the art lines produced early in the Brush-McCoy period were Venitian Ware, very similar to Roseville Persian, Woodland, and Navarre. Navarre was created from molds of Owens' Henri Deux Art Nouveau figures, with a dark green semi matt glaze filling in the surface between the figures.

On March 9, 1912, the Directors received a proposal to buy the A. Radford Company of Clarksburg, West Virginia, for $3,000. But as the location of the plant was felt to be unsuitable, they rejected this offer. However, at their April meeting the "Manager presented a new proposition from A. Radford Pottery Company offering to sell molds, saggers, and (established business and other items) for $2,000." This plan was investigated, and the purchase was unanimously approved.

We can surely assume that the Brush-McCoy Company bought the Radford molds with the intent of putting them to use, but no attempt was made to reproduce Radford's lines. There are vase shapes, for instance, that appear in Brush-McCoy lines with their own glazes that appear to be identical to some of the Radford shapes. But none of the Radford "figure molds" were included in the purchase, and as far as is known, none were ever used by any other pottery.

Late in November 1914, J. W. McCoy became gravely ill. At the December 9th Board of Directors meeting, Mr. Brush made a motion to express concern to Nelson McCoy in the serious illness of his father. Two days later, on December 11, J. W. McCoy was dead of anemia at the age of 66. After his father's death, Nelson McCoy continued to represent the family's interest, serving as a member of the Directorate until 1918.

On November 28, 1914, the Brush-McCoy Pottery Company filed an application for registration of this trademark: M-I-T-U-S-A, a composite of the first letter of each word in the phrase "Made-In-The-United-States-(of)-America." The trademark was registered on June 8, 1915, and was to remain in use by the company for ten years. Although evidently intended for use on the ware, none has been found bearing this mark.

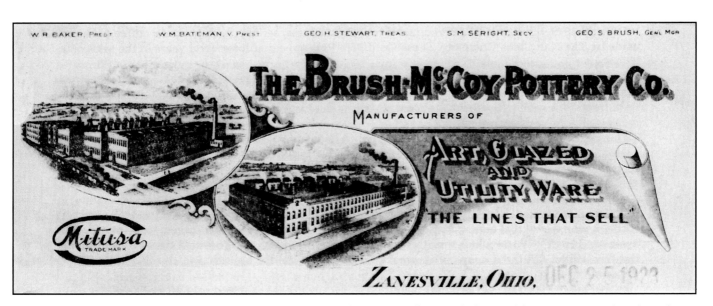

*This letterhead was in use from 1915 to 1924, with revisions necessitated by changing officers. Both plants and the M-I-T-U-S-A trademark are shown.*

George Brush was a co-founder of the Associated Glass and Pottery Manufacturers Show and served as its treasurer until his death in 1934. The first of these shows was held in 1917 at the F. T. Pitt Hotel in Pittsburgh. In later years, they were located at the Wm. Penn Hotel. Frank Vaughn and Ed Downey were two of the first salesmen to work with the displays, followed some years later by Gerry McConnell, who was sales manager and a director, and W. Clare Barnett, later to become president of the firm. In 1930, one of the company's large frog lawn ornaments greeted visitors at the booth, and thus a tradition was established that continued for many, many years.

Although the Roseville plant had been advertised for sale in 1916, it had not sold. The fact that they still owned this second pottery proved to be a deliverance when on November 9, 1918, fire broke out in the kiln sheds of Plant No. 1 in Zanesville and communicated to the manufacturing departments. Only the office buildings which were saved by a fire wall remained. The fire burned from sometime after 11 o'clock on Saturday night until 8 o'clock on Sunday morning. Loss was estimated at $100,000, and the jobs of 96 employees were affected.

At the December 11, 1918, meeting of the board, Nelson McCoy resigned as a director, and John Taylor, foreman of the shipping department in Plant No. 2 at Roseville, was elected to replace him. The other directors were re-elected: W. R. Baker, George Stewart, Wm. Bateman, and George Brush.

In January 1919, a church lot adjoining Plant No. 2 in Roseville was purchased, improvements were made in the pottery, and more gas-fired round kilns were built to accommodate the increased production. The gray stone body of the art ware produced at this location can easily be distinguished from those earlier lines produced in Zanesville, which are lighter in weight and ivory in color. Examples of these stoneware art lines are Florastone, Jewell, Jetwood, Zuni-art, King Tut, and others.

In April 1919, the company entered into a jobbing business, selling china teapots, coffeepots, etc., made by the Hall China Company. These Gardinere Pots appeared for several years in the sales catalogs.

Until 1921 when the company began the practice of paying their employees by check, often Mr. Brush would wrap money in a newspaper to avoid suspicion and with his daughter Lucile would ride the train from Zanesville to the Roseville plant to deliver the payroll. Today Mrs. Clare Barnett, Lucile has many such fond memories of her father.

During the next years improvements continued to be made — a brick building 40' x 50' x 20' high replaced the frame straw shed; a second story was added to the clay shed; the #1 kiln was torn down for casting room space; and a new boiler was added. In 1925 a new clay-working machine was purchased for $10,000.

Although it was first suggested in 1922 that the name "McCoy" should be dropped from the company name, it was agreed that action would be deferred for at least one year. The subject was not broached again until late in 1925, at which time the proposal was accepted and appropriate steps taken to change the firm's title. For three consecutive weeks the following notice appeared in the Zanesville *Times Recorder*:

> Notice of Change of Corporate Name
> To Whom it May Concern:
> Notice is hereby given that at a meeting of the stockholders of The Brush-McCoy Pottery Company, held on Wed. the 9th day of December, 1925, at the office of said company, it was, by a vote of more than three-fifths of the stockholders resolved, that the Articles of Incorporation of The Brush-McCoy Pottery Company, be resolved and the same are hereby amended so that the name of said company shall be The Brush Pottery Company.
> (signed) S. M. Seright, Secretary

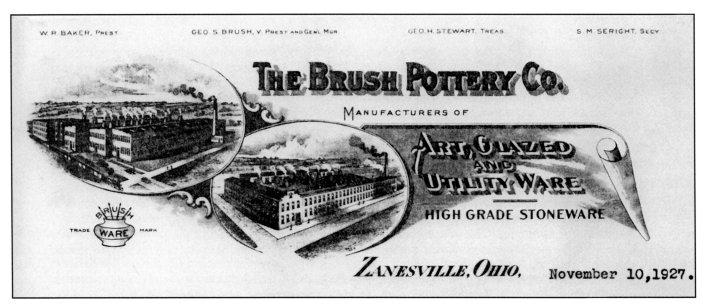

*Although this letterhead (1925 – 1933) still pictures the Zanesville plant with manufacturing portion intact, only the section containing the offices remained after the fire. Note new trademark.*

The old officers were re-elected to serve the new company at the December meeting which was held in special session at The First National Bank in Zanesville. Further business transacted at that meeting concerned the proposition to buy controlling interest in the Watt Pottery Company at Crooksville, Ohio. A resolution was presented which stated in part that "Conditions are such that it has become necessary to handle for sale a line of stoneware pottery which the company has been purchasing (for a year) for sale . . . from The Watt Pottery Company of Crooksville, Ohio," and that since "conditions are such that in the near future it may become difficult to purchase in this vicinity for resale, sufficient stoneware pottery of a satisfactory quality to meet the needs of this company. . ." it would be expedient "to have a controlling interest in said company (Watt Pottery)." One hundred and forty-five shares of the common capital stock were purchased at $100 per share. George Brush, John E. Taylor, and W. R. Baker were elected to the board of directors of the Watt Pottery. In 1927, the company authorized improvements on the Watt proper-ty for the sum of $7,000. The stoneware produced by Watt for Brush was illustrated in the sales catalogs for several years. Poultry fountains, milk feeders, churns, jugs, and water kegs carried a shield-like mark with a number denoting the capacity of the ware. This alliance continued until March 1931, when the con-trolling stock was sold back to the Watt Pottery.

In 1928, Mr. W. Clare Barnett was hired to work at the Roseville plant. He was a graduate of Ohio State University where he earned a Bachelor of Chemical Engineering degree. On October 5, 1929, Clare married Lucile Brush, his high-school sweetheart. On May 12, 1934, he was elected a director to fill the unexpired term of his father-in-law, George Brush, and in December 1944, he became vice president and assistant secretary. In 1955, Mr. Barnett became president of the pottery. He recalls his first and only attempt at modeling a line — the futuristic "Moderne" series in 1929 — and that the Onyx line that was most popular through the twenties and early thirties tended to blister in the kiln. At times his job would be to chip the blisters off the bad ware, daub on some fresh glaze, and send it through for a second firing.

Mr. Barnett pointed out the difference between the "chrome" green (which leans toward a teal shade) and the copper-green glaze known as Matt Green (new Matt Green ware was several shades lighter than the darker green we are accustomed to seeing today, since that glaze tends to oxidize over the years). He described how the Majolica umbrella stands were dipped, how the large porch jars were molded by turning the top and bottom pieces separately and then joining them at the shoulder. He identified ware modeled by Cusick during the years after 1928 and indicated earlier lines he felt reasonably sure were Cusick's work. Needless to say we enjoyed the time we spent talking with Mr. Barnett very much. They have one son, William Brush Barnett, who began working at the factory in 1949, the third generation to carry on the family tradition. He was vice president for sales in 1972, and soon after replaced his father as president of the company. Mr. Clare Barnett then served as chairman of the board of directors.

The company continued to improve and expand their facilities, and in September 1929, they built an addition to the Roseville plant and installed a tunnel kiln, purchased from the Harrop Ceramic Service Company of Columbus, Ohio, for approximately $43,000. Tom Watt, one of the brothers who owned the Watt Pottery Company, became plant superintendent, replacing Sam Pace, who had previously held that position (1913 – 29).

In 1933, Local #135 of the International Brotherhood of Operative Potters was organized with Richard Marshall as the first president, Carl Sagle as financial secretary, and Carnet Colburn as recording secretary. The union became a closed shop in 1936.

Even during these Depression years, business was on the increase. In 1934, the #6 kiln was torn down to allow more stock space, and a few years later the #4 kiln was dismantled to gain space for production. The old kiln shed was enlarged and a water system installed. In 1937, a new casting conveyor was added.

George Brush died on February 25, 1934, after a lengthy illness. Resolutions adopted by the Directors at the March meeting read in part as follows:

> Whereas, Almighty God in His Wisdom has seen fit to take from us our valued friend, counselor and fellow worker . . . Resolved, that we hereby desire to express our appreciation of Mr. Brush as a public man, and a private friend; we always found him ready to extend a helping hand in any good public or private enterprise. We learned to esteem him highly for his many kind acts, helpful suggestions and energetic work, for his active interest in the support of the religious and charitable interest in the city.

These were the officers that served the company after Mr. Brush's death: President, Robert Baker; Vice President, John Taylor; Secretary, Treasurer, and General Manager, S. M. Seright; Director (replacing Geo. Brush), W. Clare Barnett.

During the 1930s Brush Pottery was sold and distributed through a firm called the Carson Crockery Company, who advertised the ware as "Coronado Art Pottery."

In 1938, the company initiated the practice of marking their better ware with the firm name and USA. Many variations appear to have been in use.

*Letterhead in use 1934 – 1965.*

The early 1940s were a time of unrest, and due to the government's defense program, some material needed for production became at best hard to get. In some cases, shipments were delayed; others were restricted. Gas supplies were considerably curtailed, which resulted in reduced production of 20% to 25%. At home, management and union clashed. After a strike which lasted five weeks, a compromise settlement was reached with the help of the Government Concilatory Board. The draft created many vacancies within the pottery, and as each serviceman was drafted, they were sent on their way with a bonus of an extra week's pay.

By January 1945, their supply of gas had been cut in half, which naturally caused an equivalent drop in production. By March gas and production was cut by a less severe 30%. In 1946, new equipment was added, the old steam engines and boilers were replaced with electric power and gas heaters. Five more casting machines were added. During the 1950s and 1960s, the company manufactured a complete line of ware for florists, as well as commercial art ware such as wall pockets, novelty planters, and ashtrays. From the late 1940s until 1972, the company produced well over fifty different cookie jars, several of which were designed by "The Twin-Wintons" — twin brothers who left the pottery in the sixties to work in California. (You may see some cookie jars which carry their incised name and notice a very marked similarity to some they designed for Brush.)

The officers and directors of the company at the time of closing were: Wm. Brush Barnett, President; Harold Hayes, Vice President for Sales; Samuel Allen, Treasurer; Attorney John Ringhisen, Director; and Mrs. Lucile Barnett, Director and Secretary of the Board of Directors.

The hand-decorated frogs and turtles, first modeled from live specimens in 1930, remained in production for many years, made much the same as they were initially, though molds used for the later ones contained fewer pieces. During the seventies, they produced a complete line of planters, flower arrangers, pots, and vases for the florist trade. Their sales catalog cover from that period speaks eloquently of the years the company had spanned — their current ware displayed in the foreground before a photo of George Brush at his desk, the year, 1905.

# TRADEMARKS

How sad that so few of the early art ware lines were marked. But as you become familiar with the various unmarked lines, you will learn that each is distinctive enough to enable you to be confident in your identification. We have observed that so many pottery buffs learn to find clues as to manufacturer by noting the appearance of the bottom. Although different techniques were used on this ware (we have three distinctly different types in the Majolica "Amaryllis" line), it seems that most often the bottom shows a very evenly applied base color and impressed shape numbers of three digits.

One of the earliest art lines, Mt. Pelee, 1902, was marked in incised block lettering. After 1905, a steel die was used to stamp Loy-Nel-Art ware with the name of the line and the pottery. Olympia and Rosewood were both marked with the line name incised over a large M with a C superimposed over the center angle (this C looks very much like an O). Renaissance is a very rare line of the same period and is marked in the same manner as the latter two lines. Navarre, 1912, is ink stamped with a very distinctive and amusing character — a little Frenchman striding along the top of a shield-like outline containing the line name in block letters and fleurs-de-lis. In 1916, Vogue carried the ink stamped line name and Brush-McCoy and Co., Zanesville, Ohio, enclosed within the elongated oval. Although the M-I-T-U-S-A trademark adopted in 1915 was evidently originally intended to be used directly on the ware, we have yet to see a piece with this mark.

In 1938, a resolution was passed to begin the practice of marking the better art ware. Only a few of the different trademarks are shown here — there will be slight variations from piece to piece. Later, in 1967, a policy was adopted that the ware be marked with a number, so that the first two digits would indicate the year.

Gold and Black paper label,
1930s – 1940s

Late 1920s – ?

Gold paper label, 1930s – late
1950s

u S A

1940s – mid-1950s

BRUSH
u S A

1938 – 1950s

BRUSH
USA

1938 – 1950s

BRUSH
USA
609

1938 – 1965

Late 1940s – 1960s

# UNITED STATES PATENT OFFICE.

THE BRUSH-McCOY POTTERY COMPANY, OF ZANESVILLE, OHIO.

TRADE-MARK FOR CERTAIN NAMED CROCKERY AND EARTHENWARE.

**104,665.**  **Registered June 8, 1915.**

Application filed November 28, 1914.  Serial No. 82,949.

## STATEMENT.

*To all whom it may concern:*

Be it known that THE BRUSH-McCOY POTTERY COMPANY, a corporation duly organized under the laws of the State of Ohio, and located in the city of Zanesville, county of Muskingum, in said State, and doing business at Dearborn street, Owens Addition, in the city of Zanesville, State of Ohio, has adopted and used the trade-mark shown in the accompanying drawing, for china bowls, platters, plates, cups, saucers, vases, ewers, pots, and earthenware bowls, except closet-bowls, cuspidors or spittoons, culinary utensils, dishes, basins, funnels, hearths, jars, jugs, mugs, plates, platters, pots, vases, combinettes, chambers, jardinières, pedestals, umbrella-stands, and towel-urns, in Class No. 30, Crockery, earthenware, and porcelain.

The trade-mark has been continuously used in the business of said corporation since November 14th, 1914.

The trade-mark is applied or affixed to the goods by stamping the same on the bottom of each piece of ware.

THE BRUSH-McCOY POTTERY COMPANY,

By W. R. BAKER,

*President.*

## DECLARATION.

State of Ohio, Muskingum county, s.s.

W. R. BAKER, being sworn, deposes and says that he is president of the corporation, the applicant named in the foregoing statement; that he believes the foregoing statement is true; that he believes said corporation is the owner of the trade-mark sought to be registered; that no other person, firm, corporation or association, to the best of his knowledge or belief, has the right to use said trade-mark in the United States, either in the identical form or in any such near resemblance as might be calculated to deceive; that said trade-mark is used by said firm in commerce among the several States of the United States; that the description and drawing presented truly represent the trade-mark sought to be registered, and that the specimens show the trade-mark as actually used upon the goods.

W. R. BAKER.

Subscribed and sworn to before me, a notary public, this 21st day of November, 1914.

[L. s.]  ISAAC HUMPHREY,

*Notary Public.*

Copies of this trade-mark may be obtained for five cents each, by addressing the " Commissioner of Patents, Washington, D. C."

# LINES OF MANUFACTURE

The dates we have listed below indicate the first year the line appeared in the catalog, and as there were several years from which no catalogs were available, these dates are approximate.

Early 1900s **Blended Glazed Pots and Pedestals, Umbrella Stands, Cuspidors** – Finely modeled decorations in blended glazes.

Early 1900s **Fire Clay Cooking Ware** – Bristol-glazed crockery, sometimes lined in blue.

Early 1900s **Stoneman Butter Jars** – Stoneware.

Early 1900s **Combinets and Chambers** – Plain white, blue tint, green stippled, Green-on-Ivory, and Blue Banded on standard shapes.

Early 1900s **Red Burned Flowerpots and Saucers** – In graduated sizes.

Early 1900s **Rosewood** – Standard brown-glazed ware on simple shapes, decorated only with diagonal orange streaks.

1902 **Mt. Pelee** – Molded ware that has been altered while in the wet state by pinching and pulling the clay to form peaks and crests. Most commonly found in an iridescent gray, mat green has been reported — other colors are possible.

1904 **Green-on-Ivory** – Spongeware-type utility ware, mixing bowls decorated with an overall pineapple embossing.

After 1905 **Loy-Nel-Art** – Standard brown ware, hand decorated under the glaze with colored slip, usually on simple shapes with a floral motif. A second type is noted in mat green with incised decorations — none has been located to date.

After 1905 **Olympia** – Beautifully modeled brown-glazed art ware decorated in natural colors with wreaths of leaves and berries or simple floral sprays in low relief. Some pieces are further enhanced by diagonal orange brush streaks on the reverse.

After 1905 **Rosewood (Second Line)** – Very similar to Olympia.

After 1905 **Renaissance** – Very rare brown-glazed artist-decorated ware of superior quality.

1910 **Red Onyx** – Jardinieres, pedestals, umbrella stands, etc., in high-gloss glaze of rich colors in a drip effect.

(You will find there are two shades of brown onyx, a chocolate brown and a much lighter shade. More than likely this lighter brown is the red onyx.)

1910 **Liberty Bell** – Umbrella stand, with Independence Hall on back, Liberty Bell embossed on the front. 21" high, in blended glaze, designed and signed by Cusick.

1910 **Marble Ware** – The design is reminiscent of Greek columns; some pieces have Greek Key pattern; the glaze is an ivory marble effect.

1910 **Mat Green** – Mat green glaze on various simple, unadorned shapes — an Egyptian border design is on a 21" umbrella stand, a vase shows the Greek Key pattern, and there is a footed Egyptian jardiniere with sphinx and pyramids.

1910 **Old Ivory Ware** – Finely embossed and modeled, the body is ivory with a creamy glaze. The modeling is brought out with rich brown in the incisions and around the embossed work.

1910 **Corn Line** – A fine cream body, highly glazed in natural colors of green and yellow, in tankards, pitchers, creamers, steins, cereal jar, spice jar, butter jar, tobacco jar, and salt box. Signed by Cusick.

1910 **Decorated Pitchers** – Natural colors on ivory or blue decorated on Bristol glaze. Corn, Tulip, Daisy, Copenhagen (daffodil), Iris, Holland jug (fancy shape, decorated with three daisies), Indian Village, with matching mug.

1910 **Frog Cuspidor** – Finely modeled frog on front and back with green predominating.

1910 **Blue Mottled, Blue Mottled and Banded** – Sponge-ware type decoration on ivory background, domestic ware.

1910 **Billy Possum Money Bank** – Figural money bank, 5½", in green and brown glaze.

1910 **Baby Mug** – Cream inside with blue exterior, the mug has two large handles and is decorated with the word "Baby."

1910 **Blue Stenciled Ware** – Utility ware — rolling pin, stirring bowls, jug, hanging salt box, and butter pot — in ivory Bristol glaze decorated with stenciled floral motif or simple decorative pattern.

1910 **Blue Banded Ware** – Utility ware, such as shoulder bowls, bread jar, etc., in ivory with blue bands.

1910 **Butter Jars** – Blue decoration on ivory glaze in various designs: Daisy; Holland (Dutch kids); Indian (embossed scene with two Indians and fawn).

1912 **Grape Ware** – High glazed utility ware with lattice background in white with blue grapes and green leaves, brown shading around top and green around bottom. Also in mat white.

1912 **Venetian Ware** – Horizontal bands of deep gold separated by wide creamware bands decorated with stylized floral patterns utilizing pouncing technique (very similar to Roseville Persian).

1912 **Decorated Ivory Woodland** – Tall trees with fence in background is embossed in wide, horizontal center panel. When a top panel is added, it is of flying geese. The bottom panel which shows rabbits is used only on larger pieces. The mat glaze is deep gold with ivory highlights and green bands.

1912 **Green Woodland, Brown Woodland** – Same pattern, but in a high gloss glaze in solid colors.

1912 **Oriental Ware** – Embossed creamware shading from cream to red with various garden scenes executed in black.

1912 **Navarre Faience** – Green backgrounds with incised Art Nouveau figures in white — made from Owens' Henri Deux molds.

1912 **Cobalt Blue Line** – Jug, cat soap slab, cuspidor, Baby line — two-handled mug, bowl, pitcher, and plate — in cobalt blue with gold trim.

1915 **Cleo Vases** – Simple shapes are decorated in bright colors with stylized floral or geometric designs on ivory backgrounds with shaded borders of various hues, similar to Roseville Persian.

1915 **Agean Inlaid** – On standard company shapes embossed with the Greek Key motif in green with white accenting pattern.

1915 **Oakwood** – Wood effect finish, trimmed with a stenciled border, and molded in bars that simulate a metal holder or stand.

1915 **Blue Bird** – Ivory backgrounds are decorated with three flying blue birds, with rose-colored accents at the rim and base on simple shapes.

1915 **Baby Line** – Mug, bowl, and pitcher in ivory with red bands, animal figures, and word Baby.

1915 **Roman Decorated** – Horizontal bands of deep gold or green separated by wide contrasting panels decorated by means of pouncing, with scenes of ancient Rome — chariots and lions.

1915 **Flora** – Wide horizontal center panel is decorated with repetitive border of stylized flowers, in Salmon, Canary, Umber, Maroon, or Green.

1915 **Beautirose Ware** – Embossed shapes featuring a central and bordering rose pattern on ivory backgrounds with green highlighting and red roses.

1915 **Dresden Ware** – Embossed shapes with pointed vertical panels alternating from solid green to ivory with red roses on ivory backgrounds.

1915 **Decorated Autumn Oak Leaf** – A jardiniere and pedestal is shown, embossed with naturalistic autumn oak leaves with a small squirrel visible among the foliage — the base has a bark-like appearance.

1915 **Basket Ware** – Woven basketweave bottom with a wide border at the top decorated with clusters of grapes, vines, and leaves. Shown in "Ivotint," ivory accented by rich gold in the embossed work, green leaves and vines, and pink grapes. This glaze treatment is later called "Peach Bloom Ivotint," and is used on Amaryllis shapes.

1916 **Basket Ware** – Same line as 1915, shown in blended glazes of green and brown high gloss.

1916 **Novelty Grass Growing Hobo Head and Pig**

1916 **Money Banks** – Hobo, Pig, Frog

1916 **Bon-Ton** – Mat glazed, embossed ivory ware decorated in green and brown tints. Two styles are shown: (1) panels of long-stemmed tulips alternate with pea-pod decoration, filigree border around top. (2) Embossed grape-and-leaf motif decorates wide horizontal band in center.

1916 **Vogue** – Greek Key and/or Column design on stark white backgrounds with black, green, or gold emphasizing the pattern.

1916 **Nurock** – Quality utility ware in yellow and brown glaze, similar to Old English Rockingham.

1916 **Dandyline** – Yellow kitchen ware trimmed with white bands.

1916 **Willow Ware** – "White-Stone" Bristol glaze, shaded with blue top and bottom, in a basket-weave design, sometimes a floral spray was added.

1916 **Peacock** – Peacock at at the fountain embossing on Nurock and/or blue and white ware.

1916 **Cooking Ware** – Crocks, baking dishes, pie pans, etc., in yellow ware, with blue lined interior.

1916 **Decorated Pitchers** – Iris, Old Mill, Amsterdam (Kissing Dutch kids), Tulip, Copenhagen (daffodil), Fleur-de-Lis. Shown in natural colors on ivory, solid green or brown, or in blue and white.

1916 **Sylvan** – Embossed creamware with knarled trees whose leaves form the top edge of the ware with green and brown tints accenting the pattern.

1916 **Cuspidor** – Shown in various glaze treatments: cream with green bands; cobalt blue with gold festoons; or cream ware with green band over row of wreaths.

1916 **Our Lucile Toilet Set** – (Named for daughter of George Brush.) Stoneware in ivory Bristol glaze shaded with blue and decorated with an embossed bow knot and floral decal.

1916 **Decorated Dandyline** – Yellow ware trimmed with white enamel bands featuring flying blue bird decoration.

1917 **Birds, Bees, Butterflies, Bowls, Bird Baths, Etc.** – Ornamental pottery for table and garden.

1918 **Bruco Toilet Set** – Embossed creamware, decorated with green shading and floral decal in natural colors.

1918 **Arbor Condiment Set** – Cereal jars, spice jars, salt box, oil or vinegar bottle, with lattice background in white, decorated with cluster of blue grapes and green leaves.

1918 **Old Mill Condiment Set** – White background decorated with windmill scene.

1918 **Patriotic Bee** – Red, white, and blue bee made for coat lapel or lady's hat.

1918 **Uncle Sam Hat** – Red, white, and blue match or toothpick holder.

1918 **Vista** – Parading white ducks on a green background under a blue sky and white clouds, framed at the rim by the tree tops. Ducks are omitted on the hanging basket.

1918 **Lotus** – Vertical pointed ivory panels on green or gray background.

1918 **Monochrome** – Embossed design in neutral gray with borders of flying white birds.

1920 **Mat-Glaze Ware** – Beautiful tints of green, brown, and cream on shapes that vary from standard company shapes to those with classic modeling, featuring panels, drapery, festoon, and vines.

1920 **Pompeian** – Artistically modeled in a rich brown body with a semi-mat finish inlaid with Verde Green – very similar to Peters and Reed, Moss Aztec.

1920 **Oriental Vases** – Simple shapes done in blended effects of blue, tan, and brown — often mistaken for Peters and Reed Landsun.

1920 **Chromart** – Hand-painted scenic line featuring road leading between trees into snow-capped mountain peaks — same coloration and glazes as Oriental vases, very similar to Chromal.

1920 **Perfection ware** – Cooking ware in brown body, brown with white lining.

1921 **Newmat** – Apple green, orange, or royal blue on simple shapes; soft glazes.

1922 **Colorcraft Bristol Stoneware** – Bristol white with brown and blue decoration.

1923 **Stonecraft** – White stone body with glazed interiors, colorful decorative border in high relief.

1923 **Onyx** – Simple shapes in high glaze with richly blending colors in shades of either green, blue, or brown.

1923 **Jetwood** – Shaded bisque-like background in neutral colors, hand decorated in either high gloss or flat black scenes representing twilight in the woodland.

1923 **Zuniart** – Clay body decorated with horizontal bands of Indian designs in colorful glazes.

1923 **Art Vellum** – Simple shapes in soft colored glazes resembling ancient parchment.

1923 **Nuglaze** – Jardinieres with embossed design featuring either roses and masques or grapes, in rich tricolored combinations.

1923 **High-Gloss** – Jardinieres with embossed designs of roses and masques, in solid colors of high-gloss glazes.

1923 **Jewell** – Shaded bisque-like exteriors decorated with high-gloss design. Triangular voids within rose-red triangles form border under rows of blue and white dots, squeeze-bag technique.

1923 **Egyptian** – Dark brown glaze with green antiquing on standard jardiniere shapes.

1924 **Panelart** – Paneled sides with trees, flowers, or other designs in alternating panel only. Some bowls are shown with the pattern that forms a border at the rim. In deep gold and/or chrome green.

192(?) **King Tut** – Stoneware art line; featuring Egyptian figures in heavy slip on bisque background, chrome green on either side of center area.

1924 **Florastone** – Stoneware background decorated in high gloss with stylized floral design in rich hues of blue and rose with white accents, under arcs and rows of dots.

1924 **Krackle-Kraft** – Simple shapes in white glaze with blue crackle effect, which only rarely forms an identifiable image.

1924 **Colonial Mat** – Simple shapes with vertical panels forming sides, in mat colors of green, fawn, and blue.

1926 **Grecian** – Green or brown stonecraft finish on "Nuglaze" shapes.

1926 **Majolica** – High-glaze majolica finish on "Amaryllis" shapes.

1926 **Pastel** – Pastel colors in semi-mat glaze on "Amaryllis" or "Nuglaze" shapes.

192(?) **High Gloss Mirror Black Teapots** – 8-oz. to 54-oz. pots, individual size has sunken cover; the body is red clay.

1926 **Salada Teapots** – Made for the Salada Company until WWII.

1927 **Stoneware** – Brown and white ware, poultry fountains, milk feeders, churns, jugs, and water kegs.

1927 **Wise Birds** – Novelty line of naturalistic owls in either soft pastel semi-mat finish or Majolica high gloss.

1927 **"Bug" door stop** – 9" beetle, supine, novelty door stop.

1927 **Bookends** – Owls, elephants, or Venetian (Indian in headdress).

1927 **Card table accessories** – Ashtray-pencilholder combinations.

1927 **Clocks** – "Jug-Time" and "Flapper" in Onyx glaze, "Owl" in either Majolica or semigloss pastel. "Sweetheart" clock shown in 1929 catalog, available in high-gloss rose-colored glaze.

1927 **Dutch** – Jug and mug set embossed with frolicking Dutchmen, in blended colors of green and brown, or high-gloss Kolorkraft hues.

1927 **Grape** – Jug and mug set embossed with cluster of grapes on lattice-effect background, brown-glazed exterior, white interior.

1927 **Mystic Radio Sets** – "Bug" offered in Onyx glaze, wall pocket in blue, green or brown, rolling pin in Dandy Line yellow.

1927 **Roman** – Various designs feature either vertical fluting or horizontal bands, sometimes both, with either garlands of flowers and lion heads or floral borders. The line is identified primarily by color and glaze treatment — either brown or green stone finish on tan unglazed backgrounds.

1927 **Kolorkraft** – Kitchen ware in vivid colors — red, blue, or green.

1928 **Florodora** – High-gloss or mat glaze, simple floral and leaf embossing on bark-like background in natural colors.

1928 **Bungalow Vases** – Large vases "for Gateways, Porticos, Walks, Conservatories, etc.," 18", 24", or 30", offered either in plain stone, Mat Green, or hand decorated at the high shoulder by a ribbon-like band and medallion featuring a central cluster of blue grapes between symmetrically placed green and gold leaves.

1928 **Athenian** – Bronze finish used on a variety of standard shapes.

1928 **Moderne Kolorkraft** – Moderne refers to the futuristic lines of the ware, while Kolorkraft indicates the glaze treatment — high-gloss Rose, Green, Orchid, or Blue — either solid colors in a mottled effect of two shades of one color or when a simple pattern is effected, the more intense shade of color is used to emphasize the lines.

1928 **Amaryllis Kolorkraft** – Amaryllis shapes feature tall, pointed leaves alternating with long-stemmed flowers, whose blooms form a border at the rim. These shapes were used with a variety of glaze treatments in other lines.

1929 **"Ye-Old-Tyme" Rockingham ware** – Casserole, custard cups, teapot, decanter and stopper, beakers (tumblers), and coasters. Similar to Nurock but without the depth of color.

1929 **Ivotint** – Rich semi-mat Ivory glaze with light green or brown highlighting the relief embossing on standard shapes from many lines — parrot wall pocket, bulb log from Floradora line, Indian bookends, and Egyptian umbrella stand.

1929 **"Modern" Blended Onyx** – High-gloss onyx finish on Stonecraft shapes.

1930 **Dandyline** – Yellow ware, now decorated with blue bands.

1931 **Pastel Kitchen Ware** – Vertical fluting sometimes augmented with a single tulip decorates utility ware offered in soft colors of green, blue, and rose.

1931 **Lawn Ornaments and Accessories** – Garden girl, fisher boy, boy on stump, various animals, owls, etc., were offered in plain stone finish, plain white finish, or decorated in natural colors. Combination fountains and birdbaths were offered in Roman or plain stone finish with decorative ornament.

1933 **Nymph** – Handled vases in mottled mat glazes of maple, rose, green, and blue.

1933 **Fawn** – Vases finished in Art Vellum glazes of blue, green, maple, or maroon.

1933 **Stoneware** – Footed shapes in plain white stone finish featuring border of lion heads and flower decoration.

1933 **Empress** – Artistically modeled, footed vases, urns, and jardinieres and pedestals, in high-gloss glazes of blue, green, rose, yellow, lavender, lime, and brown; green, brown, or blue onyx; or mat-glaze green or tan.

1933 **Vestal** – Roman influence evident in modeling, which features garlands, cameos, scroll handles, or full length "goddess of the hearth," in various combinations — finished in dual tones of subdued green, tan, and old rose mat glazes.

1933 **Rockraft** – "Modeled" from the rocks themselves, and carries all "the veins, corners, and irregularities," in stone or Moss finish.

1933 **Cameo** – Oblique fluting in horizontal bands border central panel with garlands and cameos, in both duotone mat glazes of green or tan, or in Canary Onyx, green or chocolate.

1933 **Pebble** – Pots and saucers modeled from real pebbles.

1933 **Peach Bloom Ivotint** – On Amaryllis shapes, with ivory interiors with pink and green tints accenting the pattern.

1933 **Keg Novelties** – Jug and mug set, hanging box, planters, nested bowls, etc., designed around the lines of a keg or barrel.

1939 **Swirl Oven Ware** – In dark red, green, rose, yellow, or blue.

193(?) **Sylvan** – Line of planters and vases featuring hollyhocks on mat glazes of tan or rose with green flowers, or plain white finish (second line).

1939 **Glo-art** – Artistic, softly swirled shapes with ruffled rims.

1945 **Bittersweet** – Ivory backgrounds decorated with sprigs of bittersweet in natural colors, designed by Cusick.

1955 **Cloverleaf Kitchen Accessories** – Rose and green details on ivory high-gloss glaze.

1956 **Bronze line** – Vases, flower arrangers, carafe, in beautiful bronze with drip-effect accents.

1957 **Stardust** – Soft mat glazes in shades of gray blue or high-gloss black, highlighted with white streaks.

1964 **Princess Line** – Vases and planters with elegant shapes and graceful handles decorated with curving feather shapes in shades of green and brown on ivory backgrounds. Named in honor of Princess Margaret.

Between 1933 and 1956, only a few catalogs were available for study; but even in those it was evident that the trend was changing from producing "lines" of pottery to groups of novelties and occasional pieces, etc., and the few lines produced through those years were seldom named.

# COOKIE JARS
## Descriptions and Dates of Manufacture

Several jars were used for years with change in color and glaze; we have noted these changes to help you more accurately date your cookie jar. (Those with "W" numbers were designed by "The Twin Wintons.")

**1946:**
Elephant with Monkey (designed by Cusick and Barnett)

**Early 1950s:**
W14 Teddy Bear (with feet apart)
W15 Squirrel with Top Hat
W7 Formal Pig (black coat and hat, produced through 1956)
W8 Elephant (wearing baby hat)
W10 Cow with Kitten Finial (in brown glaze)
W9 Circus Horse

**1956:**
W19 Granny Cookie Jar (plain skirt)
W17 Little Angel
W16 Raggedy Ann
W18 Humpty Dumpty with Beanie and Bow Tie (discontinued 1961)
W20 Old Clock
K23D Peter Pan (matching mug)
K25D Little Boy Blue (matching mug)
K24D Red Riding Hood (matching mug)
    Davy Crockett (matching mug)

**1957:**
W14 Teddy Bear (with feet together)
W17 Little Girl (same style as angel)
W19 Granny (added polka dots to skirt)

**1959:**
W23 Old Shoe
W24 Pumpkin with Lock on Door (discontinued in 1961)
W21 Panda
W22 Clown (wearing brown pants)

**1960:**
W25 Happy Bunny (dark bunny with white clothes)

**1961:**
W26 Squirrel on Log (brown high gloss)
W27 Laughing Hippo

**1962:**
W30 Covered Wagon
W32 Cinderella Pumpkin
W31 Cookie House (in rich colors)

W29 Humpty Dumpty with Peaked Hat (satin glaze)
W28 Treasure Chest

**1964:**
W33 Donkey and Cart (with ears up, brown glaze)
W22 Clown (wearing yellow pants)

**1965:**
W25 Happy Bunny (in white, with pastels)
W31 Cookie House (in white, with pastels)
W26 Squirrel on Log (gray log)
W7 Formal pig (reissue with yellow coat and hat)
W33 Donkey and Cart (ears down; black donkey, yellow cart)
W22 Clown (wearing pink pants)

**1966:**
W39 Puppy Police
W26 Squirrel on Log (satin glaze, gray tones)
W37 Sitting Pig
W38 Chick and Nest

**1967:**
W32 Cinderella Pumpkin (in yellow)
W42 Stylized Owl
W41 Stylized Siamese
W40 Nite Owl (satin glaze in gray)
#43D Hillbilly Frog

**1969:**
W46 Smiling Bear
W45 Sitting Hippo
W44 White Hen on Basket
W26 Squirrel on Log (light tan)

**1970:**
W51 Nite Owl (in brown)
W50 Cow with Cat Finial (in purple)
W49 Clown Bust

**1971:**
W54 Dog with Basket
W53 Antique Touring Car
W52 Fish
W55 Hobby Horse
W56 Boy and Balloons

# ROSTER OF OFFICERS, EMPLOYEES, AND ASSOCIATES

## J. W. McCOY

J. W. McCoy was born in Zanesville, Ohio, on January 24, 1848. His father, W. Nelson McCoy, was a potter and wholesale dealer in stoneware and was at one time mayor of Zanesville. J. W. McCoy was for years a leading merchant in Roseville, where he operated a general store. He stocked stoneware ink stands and fruit jars produced by Kildow, Dugan and Company. Soon he found that his interest in the pottery had intensified, and here began his career in the clay industry. He invested in the firm, which then became known as Kildow, Williams and McCoy. Aside from his valuable contribution to the trade, McCoy was highly esteemed, known for his integrity and devotion to business. He was a leader in educational development and was responsible in part for the construction of Roseville's first high school.

## GEORGE S. BRUSH

George S. Brush was a man with a multi-faceted personality — a success at everything he attempted — a self-made man. In later years, he would recount with a smile the story of how he earned his first dollar — one of two wide-eyed and no doubt nervous 10-year-old boys hired to guard the local cemetery to prevent grave robbers from stealing the bodies for colleges. In those days, medical students learned of anatomy and surgical procedures "first hand" from cadavers! George and his friend were paid 25¢ per night — split between the two of them. So began his career — from a plucky 10-year-old "grave-sitter" to the president of the Brush Pottery Company. George Brush successfully pursued many interests, made countless friends, and stood firm in his convictions. He was active in religious, civic, and philanthropic endeavors in the community.

Born in New Lexington, Ohio, on April 21, 1870, George moved to Zanesville with his family when he was nine years old and continued his schooling there until he was twelve. Then, when it became necessary for him to help support his family, he laid aside his studies and went out to find work. He was hired at a grocery store, and for a year he was employed as an errand boy. At thirteen he became first a fireman and then

*George Brush sits at his roll-top desk in the old J. B. Owens office (used by the Brush Pottery Company). Miss Nellie Mautz sits beside him; she worked as secretary for both companies and later married S. M. Seright. The other man is thought to be Frank Hartman. On the wall hangs a calendar showing the date to be 1905.*

an engineer for oil drillers in the Muskingum Valley. At fourteen, he was back in Zanesville — an errand boy, porter, and window cleaner for Sturtevant and Martin Department Store. After a few years, he became interested in the printing trade, and in 1885, he obtained employment in a local printing office where he gained much experience, working in various departments until July 1901 (and perhaps it was here we can say his career in the ceramics industry began), when he was hired by Owens to become the head of his printing department and editor of *The Owens Monthly*. From this point on, the story is a familiar one.

At the age of 16 he started a monthly newspaper called *The Independent*, published in the interest of foreign stamp and tag collectors. He wrote the text, set the type, and printed and mailed three issues. After the third issue, the Federal Post Office Department refused to carry *The Independent* as second class matter — and so came an untimely end to his paper.

George Brush loved music and was gifted with a natural talent for it. His older stepbrother was not only an accomplished guitarist but could build the instruments as well. Perhaps he taught George the fundamentals of music. At the age of 13, George was a member of a male quartet, and in his early years he sang in numerous churches. Later, with his step-brother, he sang and played the guitar in a troupe called the Natchez Quartet, entertaining travelers on the river boats. He was a member of a concert company and became seriously interested in composing. One of his compositions, "A Warm Number," was written for strings and became one of the first syncopated numbers published in 1900. He chose to use his two middle names, "Seigfried Leanidas," to identify his work, but the copyright was obtained by "George Brush." He experimented with playing a number of instruments, one of which was the xylophone. Many years later he adapted his expertise when he devised a set of "musical bowls" which he and Mr. Vaughn played over radio station KDKA — an ingenious way to advertise the Pottery Show at Pittsburgh!

Always active in his church, he sang in the choir and for many years taught the men's Bible class at the Brighton Presbyterian Church where he was a member. He served his city as councilman and director of the YMCA, a member of the Zanesville Sinking Fund, director of the William Shinnick Educational Fund, and director of the First Trust and Savings Bank. He was a member of the Amity Lodge of Masons in Zanesville.

He was respected and admired by friends and employees, and his fairness and sympathetic concern endeared him to all who knew him. He married Edith Jordan, who was herself involved in the trade — she worked for the Mosaic Tile Company, where her brother Ray Jr. once served as president and her father as foreman.

*W. Clare Barnett with new tunnel kiln, 1929.*

## WM. R. BAKER
### (President of the Board of Directors, 1905 – 1932)

From the Zanesville and Muskingum County, Ohio, history by Thomas W. Lewis:

Mr. W. R. Baker "came to Zanesville from Deavertown in 1870 and took a position in Haynes and Sturgeons Wholesale grocery house. Ever since then he has been a resident of the city for many years in the wholesale trade, later with C. Stolzenbach, and after that with the National Biscuit Company, until he organized the Baker Bread Company." In the same publication, Mr. Baker is listed as a director of five banks and savings companies.

He married Emma Louise, the daughter of Conrad Stolzenbach; they had three sons: Carl Conrad, Robert Jacob, and Frank. Carl served briefly as a director of the pottery and in 1936 succeeded John Taylor on the board, a position he held until his death on August 22, 1939. His son Alfred was elected to succeed him. Wm. Baker was listed in the minutes with Mr. C. Stolzenbach as being a major stockholder of the company; the Baker family continued to hold a major interest until 1955 when the majority of their shares were sold to the Barnett family. Robert was for a time manager of the Baker Bread Company and succeeded George Brush as president of the pottery in 1934, a position he held until the late 1940s.

## W. CLARE BARNETT

W. Clare Barnett served the pottery in many capacities. He was born on October 29, 1906, in Zanesville, Ohio. He attended Ohio State University and graduated as a chemical engineer in 1928. He was first employed by Mead Pulp and Paper Company, but soon became interested in the pottery business. He joined the company in the fall of 1928 and worked in the Roseville plant where he experimented with glazes and the control of the new Harrop Tunnel Kiln, which was installed in 1929. He managed the installation of a new conveyor system in casting and acquired a general knowledge of the manufacturing processes.

In 1934 he moved into office work, and in May of that year he was elected a director of the Brush Pottery. He served at various times as vice-president, assistant secretary, and in December 1955 he became president and general manager. In 1976, he was elected chairman of the board of directors.

*Photo of J. B. Owens Plant No. 1 as it looked after rebuilding following a fire in 1902.*

## W. B. COSGRAVE

W. B. Cosgrave was the first vice-president of the original Brush Pottery Company. He was associated with the Harper and Cosgrave Wholesale Grocery (originally Mercantile Wholesale Company) and Cosgrave Shoe Company. He was president of the Union National Bank and from 1903 – 1905 served as a member of the Ohio legislature.

## J. B. OWENS

J. B. Owens built and originally operated the pottery on Dearborn Street in Zanesville, later owned by the Brush Pottery Company. In his article "Roseville Grew Rapidly During 1890 Boom" (*Sunday Times Signal*, Zanesville, Ohio, August 2, 1959) local historian Norris Schneider reports: "After J. B. Owens had become phenomenally successful as salesman for Brown and (J.W.) McCoy, he paid $300 for a small pottery on the site of the Tycer plant in 1885, when he was only 25 years old." He moved to Dearborn Street in the Brighton section of Zanesville in 1891, where he continued to manufacture his original line of stoneware until 1896 when he began to produce fine art pottery. Owens made art ware for only ten years, after 1906 he produced only floor and wall tile there. He sold his Dearborn Street property in 1909 to Wm. Shinnick and relocated directly across the street where he continued to manufacture tile until a fire on January 7, 1930, destroyed the pottery. He also had a pottery in New Jersey, with offices in New York. The Zanesville Tile Company is recorded to have dissolved on November 16, 1936, two years after his death, although manufacturing was not resumed after the fire.

## ALBERT RADFORD

A. Radford was a master potter and one of several men whose names are briefly associated with one and then another of several local potteries. In 1901, Radford worked for J. B. Owens, not only as a modeler but as superintendent of the pottery as well. He remained with Owens for approximately two years, after which time he was involved with his father Edward Thomas Radford in building the A. Radford Pottery of Zanesville, which was built for the Arc-En-Ceil Pottery Company. Radford sold to Arc-En-Ceil in August 1903, and the following year he became general manager of the A. Radford Pottery Company in Clarksburg, West Virginia, where he remained until 1907. *On April 11, 1912, the Brush-McCoy Pottery Company bought some of Radford's molds and saggers. Although naturally some of these molds were put to use by Brush-McCoy, they did not attempt to reproduce glazes.

*From A. Radford Pottery, His Life and Works, by His Grandson: Fred W. Radford.*

## SAMUEL MELVIN SERIGHT

S. M. Seright worked for Owens in 1905 in the same office building later occupied by the Brush Pottery. He married Miss Nellie Mautz, who was also an employee of Owens at that time. They were both on the payroll of the first Brush Pottery in 1907, she as a secretary earning $7.50 per week, for six hours, six day per week; he as bookkeeper at $12.00 per week. When fire destroyed the Brush Pottery, Mr. Seright went to work for J. W. McCoy, beginning on March 1, 1909. He was shortly elected secretary of the company and in 1926 became a director, filling the post left vacant by the death of Wm. Bateman. He was elected secretary-treasurer in 1929 and in 1933, due to the ill health of Mr. Brush, became assistant manager. He became president and general manager in the late 1940s. In 1955 he became semi-retired, but continued to serve the company as chairman of the board. He was present at the December 1970 meeting of the stockholders and directors; three weeks later he was dead at the age of 88. He was at one time a director of the Watt Pottery Company and along with Clare Barnett and G. R. McConnel sold individual hot plates and wall plaques for the Mosaic Tile Company through a jobbing firm known as McConnel and Company.

## GEORGE STEWART

George Stewart was listed as treasurer of the J. W. McCoy Pottery on their letterhead as early as 1905. He remained with the company through both re-organizations, and is listed again on the Brush Pottery letterhead in 1925. He may have retained this position for a few more years — perhaps until Mr. Seright was elected secretary and treasurer in 1929. He was at one time vice-president of the First National Bank of Zanesville and served as Postmaster in 1927.

## CONRAD STOLZENBACH

C. Stolzenbach served as president of the J. W. McCoy Pottery Company from 1901 until 1905. During this period he was listed along with Wm. Baker as a major stockholder of the company. Mr. Stolzenbach owned and operated a wholesale bakery on Main Street in Zanesville, where during the Civil War, he made hard bread for the Union Army. He is known to have had one of the country's first cracker bakeries. Mr. Stolzenbach was president of the First National Bank for many years.

## A. C. TATMAN

A. C. Tatman worked at the original Brush Pottery in 1907 as plant superintendent. He was born in 1874, a native of Crooksville, Ohio. After the Brush-McCoy reorganization, he worked in the Roseville plant as foreman of the casting department. He and S. M. Seright were members of the Brighton Presbyterian Church and the men's Bible class taught by Mr. Brush and Mrs. Cusick. Mr. Tatman was also a member of the Knights of Pythias, Masons, and Modern Woodmen.

## GEORGE DOWNEY

George Downey embarked on his career as a company salesman in 1907, when he went to work for the original Brush Pottery. As was the practice in those early days of the trade, he would rent a hotel room, set up the samples, and invite customers in to see them. Mr. Downey remained with the company until he was past eighty, mainly serving Mid-West area. He remained active and vital until his death on April 15, 1969. He was ninety-eight years old.

## FRANK VAUGHN

Frank Vaughn served the company for many years as salesman for the New England area. He was a stockholder and represented the company on the Directorate of the Watt Pottery Company when the companies were associated.

## W. G. McCONNELL

W. G. McConnell worked for the company from the early 1940s until he retired about 1970. Formerly a salesman for the Watt Pottery, Mr. McConnell divided his time between the Watt and Brush Potteries as their sales manager, after the death of George Brush. In the latter 1940s, he began to work full time for the Brush Pottery and subsequently became a director. He organized a jobbing firm called McConnell and

Company and along with Mr. Seright and Mr. Barnett contracted with the Mosaic Tile Company to sell individual tiles as hot plates and wall plaque gift items.

## HAROLD HAYES
Harold Hayes served as manufacturer's representative for the Watt Pottery Company until that factory burned. In 1968, he became assistant sales manager for the Brush Pottery and later held the position of vice-president for marketing.

## GEORGE KRAUSE
George Krause worked part time (after retiring from his position as technical supervisor for the Roseville Pottery) as a ceramist for the Brush Pottery Company, where he remained active until after 1972. He was a native of Bunzlau, Germany.

## W. C. MOONEY
W. C. Mooney was president and principal stockholder of the original Brush Pottery in 1907. He was a resident of Woodsfield, Ohio, and is remembered as being active in seeking financial backing from residents of several nearby communities.

## CHARLES CHILCOTE
Chas. Chilcote is a well-known designer and decorator who worked for the J. W. McCoy Pottery Company, occasionally signing his work. It is also believed that he worked for Roseville, Owens, Weller, and Zane Potteries. Mr. Chilcote lived in Zanesville, Ohio, until his death.

## THE TWIN WINTONS
The Wintons of California designed a long line of cookie jars and other pieces identified by a W number. They left the Brush Pottery, returning to California where they continued in the business until the summer of 1977, when they sold the company.

## AL DYE
Al Dye of Williamstown, West Virginia, was responsible for most of the modeling done during the 1970s. He designed many of the cookie jars with the exception of those with the W numbers.

## LITINSKY
Litinsky (?) worked for the pottery around 1922. He worked with Mr. Cusick to develop the blue and white KrackleKraft glaze. It is believed that he escaped from Russia through Japan to get into the United States. No record of his name has been found.

## HELEN JAMISON LONGSTRETH
Mrs. Longstreth worked with Mr. Cusick, assisting him as he experimented to determine the most suitable method of decoration for each new piece of ware. She also kept records of the time each finishing operation required, so that the price per item could be established. Her father worked for Brush-McCoy from 1919 to 1959, and her husband Arthur worked for Nelson McCoy until he went into the service in the 1940s. Mrs. Longstreth began at the pottery in 1925, remaining there for 17 years.

## ALBERT LOGAN CUSICK
Perhaps one of the most familiar names from the ranks of the artisans of the glorious era of art pottery was that of Albert Logan Cusick. He was born on January 7, 1881, in Tiltonsville, Ohio, where he was reared and educated, completing all the public schooling that was available to him. After graduation he applied for a teaching certificate, passed his exam, and was granted a license to teach by the state of Ohio. But he never taught — instead the lure of the potter's wheel and the romance of the fire so captured his interests that he remained a dedicated craftsman of the trade until his death in January 1946.

Aside from a short course in ceramics at Ohio State, Cusick was self taught. He read everything he could find on pottery making, and his natural talents more than compensated for a lack of formal training. His associations with many fine potters early in his career provided him with an excellent opportunity to gain practical experience from the best in the field. His earliest venture into pottery making was in Tiltonsville. (The Vance Faience Company operated in Tiltonsville from 1900 – 1902.) By 1902, he was working with William P. Jervis who was manager of the Avon Faience Co., which replaced the Vance organization. In 1903, the Avon Pottery became part of a company called the Wheeling Pottery, and Cusick is known to have worked for a time there in Wheeling, West Virginia, until they stopped the manufacture of art pottery about 1905. He and Mr. Jervis then organized the Craven Art Pottery of East Liverpool, Ohio, and for a few years produced art pottery, experimenting with both glazes and modeling. For some reason this operation was not successful, and by 1908 Cusick had returned to Roseville, Ohio, where he began his lifelong association with the Brush-McCoy organizations as their principal designer.

Perhaps the earliest line he designed was the Corn Line. His incised name can be found on many of these early tankards and mugs, either on the lower bar of the handle or at its base. The Independence Hall-Liberty Bell umbrella stand is also signed "Cusick," and no doubt many others of these early lines can be accredited to him, although no one we talked with can recall much of these very early years. Mr. Barnett became part of the Brush Pottery in 1928, and can remember that Cusick decorated some of the large bungalow vases in the late 1920s and felt that one could attribute the "Wise Owls" to Cusick's expertise. Jay Cusick remembers his father working with a Russian with a name that sounded like "Litinsky" (the spelling is approximate since the name has never been found in company records) when they worked together to develop the KrakleKraft line of 1925.

In 1933, he created the Vestal line and in later years designed many vases, cookie jars, and animal planters. The extent of his work will probably never be fully realized. His last full line was a bittersweet design — finely modeled shapes done in a white glossy glaze decorated with sprigs of bittersweet berries and leaves in natural colors, done in 1945, one year prior to his death.

His skills were not limited to one area of work — he was an excellent designer, capable of preparing his own glazes and decorating colors, and he was expert at operating the kilns. Some of the finest examples of early art pottery bear his signature. Cusick's son Jay began part-time work with the company in 1933, full-time in 1941. In March 1969, he became superintendent of the company. We are indebted to him for recounting these early years of this well-known and highly respected artist — A. L. Cusick.

Other decorators who worked many years for the pottery are: Shelby Ditter, Hattie Spring, Zura Hicks, Mable Woods Klinger, Urla Devore Saxon, Carrie Guy, Roxie Curl, Clara Guinsler, Bertha Shipley, Bea Sisk, Mary Ungemach, Mable Charles, Elsie Marshall Sagle, Thelma Lambert.

## SECRETARIES

Miss Florence Jones of Roseville, Ohio, began working for the company in 1905. She served as secretary for every company manager, and although she worked only part-time in her later years, she was with the company until she was past eighty. She was held in high regard both at the office and in her home community.

Mary Burton Swingle served as secretary in the Zanesville office for all managers except J. W. McCoy.

# JETWOOD, 1923

You can see the highlights on the pieces decorated in the heavy high gloss black slip — these pieces are evidently more desirable and are priced accordingly.

Row 1:
    Bowl, 7½" x 2½", Shape #01 . . . . . . . . . .$250.00 – 300.00
    Candlestick, 7", Shape #030 . . . . . . . .$325.00 – 400.00 pr.

Row 2:
    Vase, 10½" . . . . . . . . . . . . . . . . . . . . .750.00 – 950.00
    Vase, 12" . . . . . . . . . . . . . . . . . . . . . .600.00 – 700.00
    Candlestick, 10¼", Shape #032 . . . . . . .400.00 – 550.00 pr.

Row 3:
    Jardiniere, 7¼" . . . . . . . . . . . . . . . . . .350.00 – 400.00
    Jardiniere, 9" . . . . . . . . . . . . . . . . . . . .600.00 – 700.00

# FLORASTONE, 1924

Row 1:

Vase, 6", Shape #077  . . . . . . . . . . . . . . . .$350.00 – 500.00
Jug, 10"  . . . . . . . . . . . . . . . . . . . . . . . .800.00 – 1,200.00

# JEWELL, 1923

Row 2:

Vase, 3"  . . . . . . . . . . . . . . . . . . . . . . . . .300.00 – 400.00
Bowl, 2½", Shape #055  . . . . . . . . . . . . . .250.00 – 350.00

Row 3:

Jardiniere, 7"  . . . . . . . . . . . . . . . . . . . . . .500.00 – 600.00
Jardiniere, 7½"  . . . . . . . . . . . . . . . . . . . . .600.00 – 700.00

# ZUNIART, 1923

Row 1:

      Moccasin . . . . . . . . . . . . . . . . . . . . . . . .$750.00 – 1,000.00

      Bowl, 7" x 2" . . . . . . . . . . . . . . . . . . . . .350.00 – 450.00

      Bowl, 5" x 2" . . . . . . . . . . . . . . . . . . . . .250.00 – 325.00

Row 2:

      Candlestick, 10", Shape #032 . . . . . . . . .600.00 – 900.00 pr.

      Vase, 10" . . . . . . . . . . . . . . . . . . . . . . . . .550.00 – 800.00

Row 3:

      Jardiniere, 9", Shape #240 . . . . . . . . . . . . .700.00 – 800.00

# ZUNIART, 1923

Top:

    Plaque, 11½" diameter ............$1,500.00 – 1,800.00

# PATRIOTIC BEE, 1918

Bottom,
Left:

    Lapel Pin ..........................600.00 – 750.00

# RADIO BUG, 1927

Bottom,
Right:

    Bug Radio, 9½" x 3" .................500.00 – 750.00

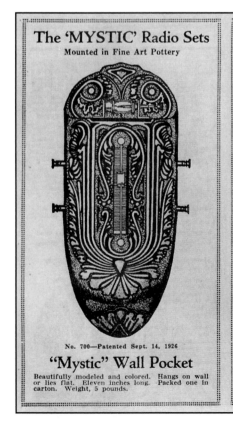

**The 'MYSTIC' Radio Sets**
Mounted in Fine Art Pottery

No. 700—Patented Sept. 14, 1926

**"Mystic" Wall Pocket**

Beautifully modeled and colored. Hangs on wall or lies flat. Eleven inches long. Packed one in carton. Weight, 5 pounds.

**The 'MYSTIC' Radio Sets**

HERE'S A GENUINE

NOVELTY SET

No. 701 "Mystic"

**ROLLING**

**PIN**

Just like every good cook uses. Yellow glazed pottery with polished wood handles. Fifteen inches long. Mounted in it is a complete Crystal Radio Set—one that will bring in local stations loud and clear.

**EVERY FAN WANTS ONE**

No. 701 Set.
Packed one in carton—weight 5 lbs.

Order through distributors or direct

**The 'MYSTIC' Radio Sets**
Mounted in Fine Art Pottery

No. 702—Patent Applied For

**"The Radio Bug"**

Nine inches long. Beautifully modeled and colored, fitted with good Crystal Set. Assorted colors. Packed one in carton, weight 5 lbs.

# IVOTINT, 1929

Row 1:
        Oil Lamp, 8" x 4" . . . . . . . . . . . . . . . . . . . .$450.00 – 600.00

# MT. PELEE, 1902

Row 2:
        Divided Tray with Handle, 7" x 2" . . . . . . . .400.00 – 650.00

Row 3:
        Console Bowl, 12" x 3½" . . . . . . . . . . .2,500.00 – 4,000.00

# KING TUT, 1923 (?)

Row 1:

Candlestick, 10", Shape #032 . . . . . . .$850.00 – 1,200.00 pr.

Vase, 12" . . . . . . . . . . . . . . . . . . . . . .1,600.00 – 1,850.00

This magnificent example of the line is personalized with this inscription:

E.M.

"RED"

7-10-23

It was decorated by Mr. Carl Sagle, who was at that time a jig-german, for the woman who was soon to become his wife, Miss Elsie Marshall.

Row 2:

Vase, 8", Shape #604 (1920s) . . . . . . . . . . .350.00 – 450.00

Vase, 7", with sailboats (1920s) . . . . . . . . .500.00 – 800.00

Panelart Vase, 8", 1924 . . . . . . . . . . . . . . .600.00 – 800.00

# NAVARRE, 1912

Row 1:

      Vase, 9" . . . . . . . . . . . . . . . . . . . . . . . . . . . .$500.00 – 750.00

# KRAKLE-KRAFT, 1924

Row 2:

      Vase, 8" . . . . . . . . . . . . . . . . . . . . . . . . . . .475.00 – 600.00
      Vase with Dragon, 10" . . . . . . . . . . . . . . .750.00 – 950.00
      Vase with Tulip, 7" . . . . . . . . . . . . . . . . . .500.00 – 700.00

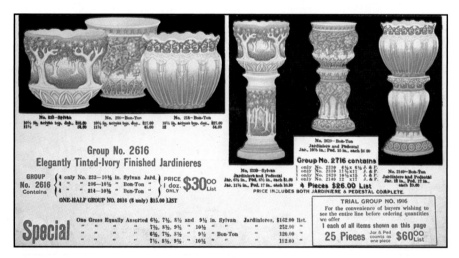

Sylvan and Bon-Ton

Row 1:

      Sylvan Jardiniere, Shape #233, 6 sizes . . . . . . . . . . . . . . . . . .$100.00 – 400.00
      Bon-Ton Jardiniere, Shape #206, 6 sizes . . . . . . . . . . . . . . . .100.00 – 400.00
      Bon-Ton Jardiniere, Shape #214, 6 sizes . . . . . . . . . . . . . . . .100.00 – 400.00
      Sylvan Jardiniere and Pedestal, Shape #2330 . . . . . . . . . . . .900.00 – 1,300.00
      Bon-Ton Jardiniere and Pedestal, Shape #2620 . . . . . . . . . .900.00 – 1,300.00
      Bon-Ton Jardiniere and Pedestal, Shape #2140 . . . . . . . . . .900.00 – 1,300.00

Row 1:

       Vase, 6", made approximately 1918,
Shape #05 . . . . . . . . . . . . . . . . . . . . . . . . . .$400.00 – 600.00
Jardiniere, 7", 1920s . . . . . . . . . . . . . . . . . . .600.00 – 800.00
Experimental Vase, 3½" . . . . . . . . . . . . .No Price Available

Row 2:

       Vase, fine white body and cobalt
decoration, 11" . . . . . . . . . . . . . . . . . . . . . .700.00 – 800.00
Vase with blue birds, 13", made
around 1915 . . . . . . . . . . . . . . . . . . . . . .800.00 – 1,000.00
Cleo Vase, 1915, 11" . . . . . . . . . . . . . . . . .400.00 – 600.00

Note: These shapes are all "Amaryllis," but three lines are represented here, distinguished by the glaze treatments.

Row 1:
"Pastel Ware" Bowl, 2", 1926 . . . . . . . . . . . .$45.00 – 60.00
"Majolica" Vase, 6½", 1926 . . . . . . . . . . . . .75.00 – 125.00
"Majolica" Candleholder, 3" . . . . . . . . . .75.00 – 115.00 pr.

Row 2:
"Egyptian" Blue Glazed Jardiniere,
5½", 1923 . . . . . . . . . . . . . . . . . . . . . . . .125.00 – 200.00
"Majolica" Vase, 4½" . . . . . . . . . . . . . . . . . .55.00 – 85.00
"Majolica" Jardiniere, 8", Shape #252 . . . . .115.00 – 200.00

Row 3:
"Pastel Ware" Jardiniere, 10", Shape #248 . .165.00 – 250.00

Amaryllis KolorKraft grouping. Vase, 9", Shape #092, $125.00 – 175.00; Jardiniere and Pedestal, 30", Shape #2520, $800.00 – 1,000.00; Candlesticks, 9", Shape #026, $150.00 – 250.00 pr.; Vase, 10", Shape #093, $175.00 – 225.00.

# VOGUE, 1916

Row 1:

       Vase, 10" . . . . . . . . . . . . . . . . . . . . . . . . .$175.00 – 250.00

       Candlestick, 12" . . . . . . . . . . . . . . . . . . . .300.00 – 450.00

Row 2:

       Jardiniere, 7" . . . . . . . . . . . . . . . . . . . . . . .175.00 – 250.00

       Experimental jardiniere has areas done in either green, black, or
gold, with metallic gold  accents.

# ONYX, 1910 – 1930s

Row 1:

      Bowl, 5" x 2½", Shape #055 . . . . . . . . . . . . .$35.00 – 75.00

      Vase, 10", Shape #041 . . . . . . . . . . . . . . . . .65.00 – 115.00

      Ashtray, 6" x 2" . . . . . . . . . . . . . . . . . . . . . .40.00 – 60.00

Row 2:

      Candlestick, 7", Shape #030 . . . . . . . . . .150.00 – 220.00 pr.

      "Jugtime" Clock, 7" . . . . . . . . . . . . . . . . .150.00 – 200.00

      Marked:

      JUGTIME

      NOVELTY ART CLOCK

      MADE IN USA

      PAT. OCT. 21, 1924

      BRUSH McCOY POTTERY CO.

      ZANESVILLE, O.

Row 3:

      Vase, 8", Shape #064 . . . . . . . . . . . . . . . . . .60.00 – 100.00

      Vase, 9", Shape #22 . . . . . . . . . . . . . . . . . . .70.00 – 115.00

      Vase, 8", Shape #064 . . . . . . . . . . . . . . . . . .65.00 – 110.00

Note: As near as can be determined, the lighter brown color was the glaze referred to as "red" onyx. Prices are higher on the green and blue items, due to their scarcity.

# ONYX, 1910 – 1930s

Row 1:

        Vase, 4" . . . . . . . . . . . . . . . . . . . . . . . . . . . . .$75.00 – 115.00

        Bottle, 10" . . . . . . . . . . . . . . . . . . . . . . . . .125.00 – 175.00

        Bowl, 6" x 2" . . . . . . . . . . . . . . . . . . . . . . . . . .35.00 – 75.00

Row 2:

        Ashtray, 5½" x 2", Shape #041 . . . . . . . . . . . .40.00 – 75.00

        Pinch Bottle, 10½" . . . . . . . . . . . . . . . . . .130.00 – 180.00

        Vase, 5½", Shape #058 . . . . . . . . . . . . . . . . . .65.00 – 85.00

Row 3:

        Candlestick, 10½" . . . . . . . . . . . . . . . . . .125.00 – 200.00 pr.

        Urn, 6" . . . . . . . . . . . . . . . . . . . . . . . . . . . . . .65.00 – 85.00

Although Onyx glazes continued to be popular in the late years of production, you will find the older Onyx to be heavier and richer in coloration.

Row 1:

    Venitian Bookends in Ivotint finish,

    5" x 5½", 1929 . . . . . . . . . . . . . . . . . . . .$200.00 – 250.00 pr.

    Bookend, "Mat-Glaze Ware,"

    5" x 5½", 1920 . . . . . . . . . . . . . . . . . . . . .180.00 – 225.00

    Venitian Bookend in Athenian Finish,

    1928 . . . . . . . . . . . . . . . . . . . . . . . . . . . .200.00 – 250.00 pr.

Row 2:

    Cuspidor, 5½", Shape #13, 1916 – 1919 . . . .150.00 – 175.00

    War Bell, 5", 1917 . . . . . . . . . . . . . . . . . . . . .65.00 – 95.00

Row 3:

    Willow Ware Cuspidor, 5½", 1916 . . . . . . . .115.00 – 175.00

    Frog Cuspidor, 5½", 1910 . . . . . . . . . . . . . .150.00 – 215.00

Onyx Frog and Bowl, $150.00 – 200.00; Amaryllis Frog and Bowl, $175.00 – 250.00; Art Vellum Frog and Bowl, $125.00 – 165.00.

Row 1:

    Decorated Cameo Jardiniere, 6",
    1933, Shape #273 . . . . . . . . . . . . . . . . . . .$150.00 – 250.00
    Lotus Jardiniere, 6", 1918 . . . . . . . . . . . . . .150.00 – 200.00

Row 2:

    Blue Birds Jardiniere, 7½", 1915 . . . . . . . . .200.00 – 350.00
    Vista Jardiniere, 8", 1918 . . . . . . . . . . . . . .400.00 – 600.00
    (Ducks on pedestal only.)

Row 3:

    Agean Inlaid Jardiniere, 10", 1915 . . . . . . . .300.00 – 400.00

Row 1:

     Stonecraft Jardiniere, 6",
     Shape #241, 1923 . . . . . . . . . . . . . . . . . . .$125.00 – 150.00
     Stonecraft Jardiniere, 7", 1923 . . . . . . . . . . .185.00 – 225.00

Row 2:

     Jardiniere with decal decoration,
     9", 1915 . . . . . . . . . . . . . . . . . . . . . . . . . . .300.00 – 415.00
     Jardiniere with hand-painted daisies,
     8½", Shape #215, 1915 . . . . . . . . . . . . . . . .225.00 – 325.00

Row 3:

     Decorated Autumn Oak Leaf Jardiniere,
     10½", Shape #29, 1915 . . . . . . . . . . . . . . . .400.00 – 500.00

Row 1:

Pompeian Window Box, 13" x 5", 1920 . . .$250.00 – 375.00

Row 2:

Blended Jardiniere, 6½", 1916 . . . . . . . . . . . .85.00 – 115.00
Colonial Mat Jardiniere, 6½", late 1920s . . .150.00 – 275.00
Note: This shape is common to the Roman line but is shown in the catalogs in this mat green glaze and designated Colonial Mat.

Row 3:

Jardiniere with Sphinx, Pyramids,
Oxen, 9", 1910 . . . . . . . . . . . . . . . . . . . . . .425.00 – 575.00

Jardiniere and Pedestal, Shape #2140, $900.00 – 1,200.00; Umbrella Stand, Shape #61, $500.00 – 650.00.

Row 1:

Sylvan Vase, 10", Shape #08, 1916 . . . . . . .$175.00 – 250.00

Note: The two lines, Sylvan and Woodland, are very similar — in fact we're not so sure the folks in 1916 could distinguish one from the other! We felt we had solved the puzzle when we determined that shapes with straight, perpendicular sides were Woodland, while Sylvan pieces were bulbous at the tree tops. Page after page in the catalogs upheld our theory, and we were just about sure we were right, when — there on one page was a vase — bulbous top, to be sure — and the line name was Woodland!

Row 2:

Sylvan Shape, stone finish, 6½" . . . . . . . . . .95.00 – 150.00
Decorated Sylvan, 7½", 1916 . . . . . . . . . . .275.00 – 450.00

Row 3:

Both of these jardinieres are experimental — the first one is decorated with birds, the second with butterflies and squirrels.

Row 1:

        Bon-Ton Jardiniere, 7", 1916 . . . . . . . . . .$150.00 – 200.00
        Jardiniere with Rockcraft finish,
        7½", 1930s . . . . . . . . . . . . . . . . . . . . . . . . . .85.00 – 140.00

Row 2:

        Jardiniere, 7½", 1916 (possibly not
        Brush McCoy) . . . . . . . . . . . . . . . . . . . . . . .65.00 – 100.00
        Basketware, 7½", 1915 . . . . . . . . . . . . . . . .95.00 – 140.00

Row 3:

        Monochrome Jardiniere, 10", 1918 . . . . . . . .250.00 – 400.00

Row 1:

      Jardiniere and Pedestal, 12", early 1900s . .$225.00 – 250.00

Row 2:

      Newmat Jardiniere, 6", 1921 . . . . . . . . . . . . .75.00 – 125.00
      Vase, in Dandyline yellow glaze, 6", 1916 . . . .50.00 – 75.00
      Jardiniere, 5½", Shape #246, 1920s . . . . . . . .65.00 – 95.00

Row 3:

      Onyx Jardiniere, 6", 1920s . . . . . . . . . . . . . .85.00 – 150.00
      Onyx Panel Jardiniere, 9", late 1920s . . . . . . .95.00 – 165.00

Row 1:

Jardiniere, 5½", 1930s . . . . . . . . . . . . . . . . . .$65.00 – 90.00

Jardiniere, 6", 1920s . . . . . . . . . . . . . . . . . . .85.00 – 115.00

Row 2:

"Glazed" Jardiniere with birds, 7",
Shape #239, 1920s . . . . . . . . . . . . . . . . . . . .75.00 – 140.00

Jardiniere, 6½", Shape #263, 1932 . . . . . . . . .85.00 – 115.00

Row 3:

Duotone Cameo Jardiniere, 10", 1933 . . . . .150.00 – 175.00

Row 1:

    Onyx Footed Urn, 9", 1920s – 1930s  . . . . .$155.00 – 225.00

Row 2:

    Pastel Ware Jardiniere, 6",
    Shape #244, 1926  . . . . . . . . . . . . . . . . . . . . .85.00 – 120.00
    Stoneware Footed Porch Urn, 8½", 1933  . . . .75.00 – 115.00

Row 3:

    Roman Jardiniere, 9", Shape #250, 1927  . . .275.00 – 350.00

Row 1:
>Globe Lamp Base, 5½", 1929 . . . . . . . . . . . . .$50.00 – 85.00
>Ivotint finish, Floradora shape,
>10" x 3", 1929 . . . . . . . . . . . . . . . . . . . . . . .$65.00 – 90.00

Row 2:
>Jardiniere, 7", 1915 . . . . . . . . . . . . . . . . . . . .60.00 – 90.00
>Blended Onyx Jardiniere, 8½", 1929 . . . . . .115.00 – 135.00

Row 3:
>Moderne KolorKraft Vase, 12", 1929 . . . . . .125.00 – 185.00
>Moderne KolorKraft Jardiniere,
>10", Shape #260 . . . . . . . . . . . . . . . . . . . . .110.00 – 165.00

Green Blended Vase, 9", Shape #042, $75.00 – 125.00; Rust Green Moderne Vase, 12", Shape #0162, $150.00 – 225.00; Butterfly Garden Ornament, rare, $100.00 – 150.00.

Row 1:

    Oriental Vase Line, 5", 1920
    (may have been made by Peters and Reed) . . .$50.00 – 85.00
    Floradora Hanging Pot, 5" x 7", 1928 . . . . . . .65.00 – 100.00
    Glo Art Vase, 3½", Shape #750, 1930s . . . . . . .50.00 – 85.00

Row 2:

    Art Vellum Vase, 8", Shape #069, 1923 . . . . . .50.00 – 75.00
    Vestal Vase, 10½", 1933, designed
    by Cusick . . . . . . . . . . . . . . . . . . . . . . . . . . .135.00 – 200.00
    Vase, "Hand decorated by Cusick,"
    8", Shape #049 . . . . . . . . . . . . . . . . . . . . .235.00 – 325.00

Row 3:

    Sylvan II Jardiniere, 4½", Shape #280, 1930s . . .25.00 – 35.00
    Sylvan II Jardiniere, 5½", Shape #280, 1930s . . .35.00 – 40.00
    Sylvan II Jardiniere, 3½", Shape #280, 1930s . . .20.00 – 30.00

Row 4:

    Vase with Shell Motif, 10", 1959, few made . . .65.00 – 100.00
    Mat Green Vase, 12", 1910 . . . . . . . . . . . . .150.00 – 200.00
    Sylvan II Vase, 10", 1930s . . . . . . . . . . . . . . .50.00 – 75.00

Back: Art Vellum Vase, 7½", Shape #718, $75.00 – 100.00; Art Vellum Jardiniere, 7", Shape #240V, $100.00 – 150.00; Vase, 12", Shape #045, $85.00 – 125.00; front: Vase, 6", Shape #048, $40.00 – 60.00; Vase, 6", Shape #746, $40.00 – 60.00.

Back Row,

Left:

   Athenian Jardiniere and Pedestal, 39" overall
   (13" jardiniere, 26" pedestal), 1928 . . . . . .$585.00 – 900.00

Right:

   Colonial Mat Jardiniere and Pedestal, 36½" overall (10½"
   jardiniere, 26" pedestal), 1927, the mold used for the jardiniere is taken from the Roman line  . . . . . .500.00 – 800.00

Front:

   Athenian Sand Jar with removable saucer,
   18", 1928 . . . . . . . . . . . . . . . . . . . . . . . . . . . .400.00 – 600.00

Jardiniere and Pedestal, Shape #2060, $600.00 – 800.00; Jardiniere and Pedestal, 26",
Shape #2020, $600.00 – 800.00; Bungalow Jar, 19", Shape #0150, $150.00 – 250.00.

Left:

Loy-Nel-Art Jardiniere and Pedestal, 27½" overall
(11" jardiniere, 16½" pedestal), Shape #205,
no mark, 1905 . . . . . . . . . . . . . . . . . . . .$900.00 – 1,200.00

Center:

Loy-Nel-Art Vase, 18", Shape #16, this is probably one of the
old Radford molds, no mark, 1912 (?) . . . . .350.00 – 550.00

Right:

Loy-Nel-Art Jardiniere and Pedestal, 25½" overall (8½"
jardiniere, 17½" pedestal), Shape #1190, no mark,
1905 . . . . . . . . . . . . . . . . . . . . . . . . . . . .1,200.00 – 1,500.00

---

Left:

Jardiniere and Pedestal, 30" overall (10" jardiniere, 20"
pedestal), hand painted, 1915 . . . . . . . . . .900.00 – 1,400.00

Second
From Left:

Flora Jardiniere and Pedestal, 28½" overall
(10½" jardiniere, 17½" pedestal), Shape #2/8,
stencil decoration, 1915 . . . . . . . . . . . . . .700.00 – 1,000.00

Third
From Left:

Sylvan Jardiniere and Pedestal, 27½" overall
(10" jardiniere, Shape #233, 17½" pedestal,
Shape #2/40), 1916 . . . . . . . . . . . . . . . . . . .700.00 – 900.00
Note: Here is where our Sylvan and Woodland lines unite! With
so little dissimilarity, these shapes must have been used
interchangeably.

Right:

Oriental Jardiniere and Pedestal, 27" overall
(9" jardiniere, Shape #211, 18" pedestal, Shape #2200),
hand painted, 1912 . . . . . . . . . . . . . . . . .1,200.00 – 1,800.00
Note: The molds used here were left in the factory from the
Owens operation.

Left:
      Blended Glazed Umbrella Stand, 19", Shape #10,
      early 1900s ........................$185.00 – 250.00

Second
From Left:
      Moss Green Umbrella Stand, 21", 1910 – 1930s . .550.00 – 850.00

Third
From Left:
      Blue Onyx Umbrella Stand, 20½", 1920s . . .400.00 – 550.00

Right:
      Loy-Nel-Art Umbrella Stand, 17½", no mark,
      1910 ...............................550.00 – 800.00

---

Left:
      Ivotint Umbrella Stand, 17", Shape #75,
      late 1920s – 1930s ....................400.00 – 600.00

Second
From Left:
      Ivotint Umbrella Stand, 21", Shape #75 ....500.00 – 650.00

Third
From Left:
      Umbrella Stand with hand-painted butterflies,
      20½", 1915 ........................900.00 – 1,200.00

Right:
      Athenian Umbrella Stand, 17", Shape #75,
      1928 ...............................400.00 – 600.00

Green Onyx group. Table, very rare, $1,500.00 – 1,800.00; Candlesticks, 10",
Shape #240, $120.00 – 140.00; Umbrella Stand, Shape #71, $500.00 – 650.00.

Left:

Onyx Umbrella Stand, 22½", Shape #74,
1910 . . . . . . . . . . . . . . . . . . . . . . . . . . . . .$450.00 – 650.00

Second
From Left:

Vogue Umbrella Stand, 22½", Shape #74,
1916 . . . . . . . . . . . . . . . . . . . . . . . . . . . . .600.00 – 900.00

Third
From Left:

Liberty Bell Umbrella Stand, 22½",
Shape #73, 1910 . . . . . . . . . . . . . . . . . . . . .800.00 – 900.00

Right:

Beautirose Umbrella Stand, 22½",
Shape #61, 1915 . . . . . . . . . . . . . . . . . . . . .750.00 – 850.00

Left:

Umbrella Stand, trimmed in gold,
22½", 1915 . . . . . . . . . . . . . . . . . . . . . . . .500.00 – 850.00

Center:

Oriental Umbrella Stand, 23", hand painted,
1912 . . . . . . . . . . . . . . . . . . . . . . . . . . . .1,200.00 – 1,500.00

Right:

Oakwood Umbrella Stand, 22½",
Shape #81, 1915 . . . . . . . . . . . . . . . . . . . . .600.00 – 900.00

Jardiniere and Pedestal, Shape #1170, $200.00 – 375.00; Umbrella
Stand, Shape #64, $185.00 – 250.00; Jardiniere and Pedestal, 17",
Shape #1340, $200.00 – 300.00.

Left:

    Oil Jar with Drip Glaze, 25½", early 1930s . . .$400.00 – 650.00

Center:

    Bungalow Vase, squeeze-bag motif, 30",

    late 1920s . . . . . . . . . . . . . . . . . . . . . . .1,200.00 – 1,800.00

    Note: Some of these were decorated by Cusick; there was also a

base shown with these in the catalog.

Right:

    Oil Jar, 24", early 1930s (18" and 30"

    also shown) . . . . . . . . . . . . . . . . . . . . . . . . . .200.00 – 250.00

———————

Left:

    Oil Jar, 12", Shape #3, 1930s . . . . . . . . . . . .95.00 – 125.00

Second
From Left:

    Oil Jar, 19", 1930s . . . . . . . . . . . . . . . . . . . .175.00 – 225.00

Third
From Left:

    Ali Baba Jar, 20", 1930s, designed

    by Cusick . . . . . . . . . . . . . . . . . . . . . . . . . .250.00 – 300.00

Right:

    Ali Baba Jar, 16½", 1930s . . . . . . . . . . . . . .200.00 – 250.00

———————

## Late 1920s through 1930s

91

**Row 1:**

Frog Birdbath Ornament, 7½", late
1920s – 1930s . . . . . . . . . . . . . . . . . . . . .$150.00 – 200.00
(much more if colored)
Frog Birdbath Ornament, 8", late 1920s – 1930s . .275.00 – 375.00

**Row 2:**

Wise Bird Decanter, 8", 1927 . . . . . . . . . . .220.00 – 300.00
Squirrel Ornament, 10", late 1920s – 1930s . . .150.00 – 200.00
Wise Bird Wall Pocket, 8", ink Brush
stamp, 1927 . . . . . . . . . . . . . . . . . . . . . . . .165.00 – 215.00

**Row 3:**

Wise Bird Bookend, 7", 1927 . . . . . . . . .200.00 – 300.00 ea.
Wise Bird Pitcher, 10", 1927 . . . . . . . . . . .200.00 – 2750.00
Wise Bird Vase, 8", 1927 . . . . . . . . . . . . . .175.00 – 250.00

**Row 4:**

Wise Bird Ornament, 9", 1927 (doorstop) . .200.00 – 300.00
Wise Bird Lamp, 9", 1927 . . . . . . . . . . . . . .195.00 – 225.00
Wise Bird Lamp, 8", 1927 . . . . . . . . . . . . . .175.00 – 200.00

**Row 1:**

Frog Bank, 3½", 1916 . . . . . . . . . . . . . . . . . .$50.00 – 75.00

Frog Flower Frog, 3", 1916 . . . . . . . . . . . . . . .65.00 – 95.00

Frog Planter, 3", late 1920s – 1930s . . . . . . . .25.00 – 40.00

Frog Bank, 3", 1916 . . . . . . . . . . . . . . . . . . . .50.00 – 75.00

**Row 2:**

Turtle Ornament 6½", 1930s . . . . . . . . . . . . . .50.00 – 80.00

Note that the green is a different shade than the later frogs, and the decoration is more detailed, rather than striped.

Double Ashtray, 6½", late . . . . . . . . . . . . . . .65.00 – 95.00

Turtle Ashtray, 5", late . . . . . . . . . . . . . . . . .40.00 – 55.00

**Row 3:**

Turtle Planter, 7", late . . . . . . . . . . . . . . . . . .30.00 – 40.00

Frog Ornament 10", 1967 . . . . . . . . . . . . . . . .65.00 – 85.00

Ornament, 4½", 1967 . . . . . . . . . . . . . . . . . . .35.00 – 50.00

**Row 4:**

Frog Ornament, 7½", 1967 . . . . . . . . . . . . . . .65.00 – 85.00

Large Ornament, 11½", 1967 . . . . . . . . . . . .150.00 – 250.00

Frog, 8", 1967 . . . . . . . . . . . . . . . . . . . . . . . .85.00 – 125.00

Note: Frogs and turtles were made by the company from the late 1920s until the company closed. Those with 1967 dates continued in production until the end.

Frog Ornament, 16", $300.00 – 400.00; Frog Ornament, 10", $65.00 – 85.00; Frog Ornament, 8", $85.00 – 125.00.

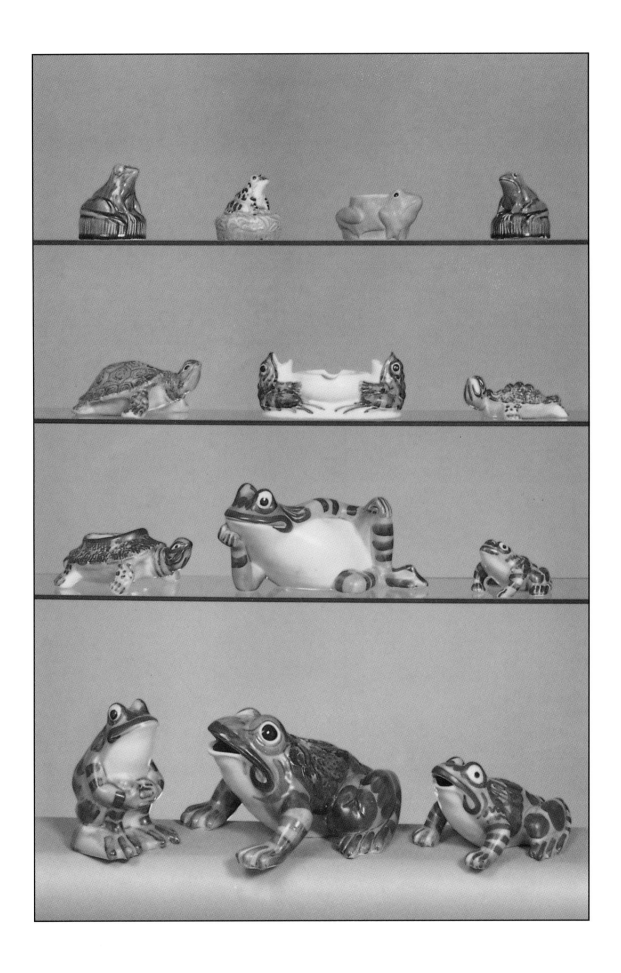

Left:

    This turtle measures 16" x 8" and has an opening on the side
    to accommodate a water hose — the spray came through the
    turtle's mouth. This is an old one, note the coloration and the
    detail, late 1920s . . . . . . . . . . . . . . . . . . . . .$600.00 – 850.00

Right:

    Frog Ornament, 22½" x 8", older shade of green,
    thick black slip on those beady eyes also help identify
    this one as old . . . . . . . . . . . . . . . . . . . . . . .600.00 – 850.00

———————————————

Bottom:

    Lucile Ware covered soap dish, possibly dating as
    far back as 1907 . . . . . . . . . . . . . . . . . . . . . .100.00 – 125.00

Row 1:

    Rolling Pin, 1910 . . . . . . . . . . . . . . . . . . . . .$125.00 – 175.00

Row 2:

    Willow Ware, 5½", "Put Your Fist In," 1916 . .100.00 – 125.00
    Willow Ware, 3", "Nutmeg," 1916 . . . . . . . .50.00 – 100.00
    Willow Ware, 6½", "Crackers," 1916 . . . . . .150.00 – 200.00

Row 3:

    Hanging Salt Box, 6½" x 4½", 1910 . . . . . . .100.00 – 150.00
    Cat Tail Pitcher, 6", 1920s . . . . . . . . . . . . . .85.00 – 125.00
    Hanging Salt Box, 4½", 1914 . . . . . . . . . . . .95.00 – 115.00

Row 4:

    Hanging Salt Box, 6½" x 4½", 1910 . . . . . . . .95.00 – 115.00
    Old Mill Pitcher, 7", 1916 . . . . . . . . . . . . . .150.00 – 175.00
    Old Mill Salt Box, 6½" x 4½", 1918 . . . . . . . .95.00 – 125.00

Row 5:

    Dutch Kids Pitcher in Nuglaze finish,
    7", 1922 . . . . . . . . . . . . . . . . . . . . . . . . . . . .135.00 – 200.00
    Kolorkraft Pitcher, 9", 1922 . . . . . . . . . . . . .95.00 – 150.00
    Amsterdam Pitcher, 7", 1916 . . . . . . . . . . .135.00 – 200.00

# NUROCK, 1916

Note: The lighter pieces were of later production, some of the smaller items such as the custard, were made up into the early 1950s.

Row 1:

      Custard, 2½", Shape #556, later manufacture . . .$25.00 – 35.00
      Butter Pat, under custard, Shape #3 . . . . . . . . . .8.00 – 10.00
      Pitcher, 4½", 1930s . . . . . . . . . . . . . . . . . . . . .40.00 – 65.00
      Bowl, 2" . . . . . . . . . . . . . . . . . . . . . . . . . . . . .25.00 – 45.00

Row 2:

      Pitcher, 5", early . . . . . . . . . . . . . . . . . . . . . .75.00 – 125.00
      Jug, 7", early . . . . . . . . . . . . . . . . . . . . . . . .125.00 – 150.00
      Cuspidor, 5", early . . . . . . . . . . . . . . . . . . . . .75.00 – 115.00

Row 3:

      Blue Mottled and Banded Cuspidor, 5", 1910 . .85.00 – 125.00
      Kolorkraft Cuspidor, 4", 1922 . . . . . . . . . . . .75.00 – 100.00
      Cuspidor, fine body, cobalt decoration,
      very early . . . . . . . . . . . . . . . . . . . . . . . . . . .150.00 – 200.00

Row 4:

      Gardinere Coffeepots, made by Hall, sold through Brush
      Pottery Company catalogs for several years,
      1919 – ? . . . . . . . . . . . . . . . . . . . . . . . . . . . . .50.00 – 75.00
      Grape Casserole, Shape #110 . . . . . . . . . . . .100.00 – 175.00  (more if colored)
      Cruet, 9½", 1910 – 1915 . . . . . . . . . . . . . . . .75.00 – 100.00

Row 1:

      Pitcher, 6½", Shape #33, 1930s . . . . . . . . . . . .$30.00 – 60.00

      Mirror Black Teapot, 4", 1920s . . . . . . . . . . . .35.00 – 65.00

Row 2:

      Brown Glaze Pitcher, 6", 1920 . . . . . . . . . . . .40.00 – 60.00

      Green-On-Ivory Bowl, Shape #195, made

      from 1904 . . . . . . . . . . . . . . . . . . . . . . . . . .15.00 – 35.00

      Mirror Black Teapot, 6", 1920s . . . . . . . . . . . .45.00 – 75.00

Row 3:

      Kolorkraft Tankard, 10", Shape #347, 1928 . .100.00 – 175.00*

      Mug, Shape #327, 1928 . . . . . . . . . . . . . . . . .30.00 – 45.00

      Keg Novelties Mug, 4", 1933 . . . . . . . . . . . . .12.00 – 20.00

      Dutch Tankard, 10", 1928 . . . . . . . . . . . . . .100.00 – 175.00

*More if multicolored glaze as is seen frequently in this pattern.

Row 4:

      Corn Pitcher, 6", Shape #44, 1910 . . . . . . . .195.00 – 250.00

      Perfection Casserole, 4" x 10", 1920s . . . . . . . .25.00 – 60.00

      Water Lily Pitcher, 5½", Shape #30, early 1930s . .55.00 – 65.00

      Note: This no doubt comes as a surprise to you McCoy (Nelson)
collectors. Both companies made this identical pitcher!

Row 1:

       Spooner, late 1950s . . . . . . . . . . . . . . . . . . . . .$35.00 – 50.00

Row 2:

       Kolorkraft Match Holder, 6", 1932 . . . . . . . . .40.00 – 65.00
       Kolorkraft Salt Box, 4½", 1932 . . . . . . . . . . .50.00 – 85.00
       Pastel Kitchenware Pitcher, 5", 1931 . . . . . . .95.00 – 195.00

Row 3:

       Dandyline Bowl, 3½" x 7½", 1916 . . . . . . . . .35.00 – 50.00
       Rainbow Kitchenware, 5" x 9½", 1930s . . . . . .30.00 – 45.00
       Kolorkraft Bowl, 2½" x 9½",
       Shape #133, 1932 . . . . . . . . . . . . . . . . . . . . .40.00 – 50.00

Row 4:

       Bowl, 4½" x 8", 1930s . . . . . . . . . . . . . . . . . .30.00 – 45.00
       Blue Banded Bowl, 6" x 10", 1930s . . . . . . . . .30.00 – 55.00
       Shoulder Bowl, 4" x 7½", Shape #175,
       1930s . . . . . . . . . . . . . . . . . . . . . . . . . . . . . .25.00 – 35.00

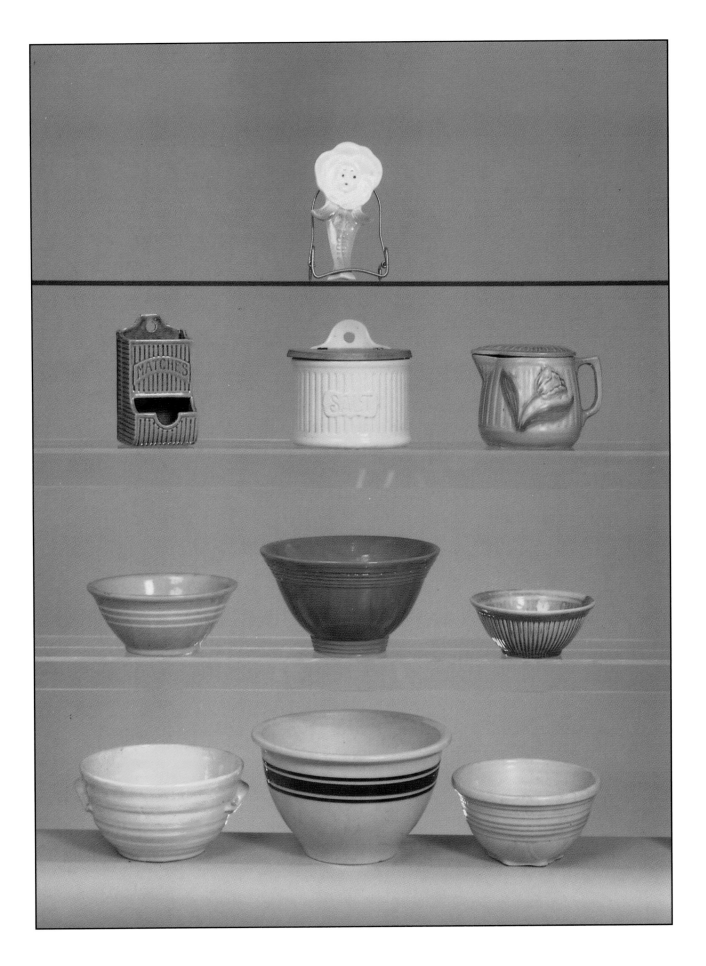

Row 1:

    Squirrel on Log, gray log – 1965, W26 . . . .$75.00 – 100.00

    Nite Owl, gray satin glaze – 1967, W40 . . . . .80.00 – 115.00

Row 2:

    Teddy Bear, feet together – 1957, W14 . . . . .150.00 – 200.00

    Panda Bear, 1959, W21 . . . . . . . . . . . . . . . .175.00 – 250.00

Row 3:

    Hillbilly Frog, 1967, #43D

    (watch for reproductions) . . . . . . . . . . .4,200.00 – 4,500.00

    Happy Bunny, white with pastels – 1965,

    W25 . . . . . . . . . . . . . . . . . . . . . . . . . . . . .175.00 – 225.00

    Note: Beware of increasing reproductions!

Row 1:

      Cinderella Pumpkin, 1962 issue shown,
      W32 . . . . . . . . . . . . . . . . . . . . . . . . . . . . . . .$175.00 – 200.00
      Old Clock, 1956, W20 . . . . . . . . . . . . . . . . .135.00 – 165.00

Row 2:

      Formal Pig, early 1950s – 56; W7 . . . . . . . .300.00 – 350.00
      Elephant with Monkey Finial, 1946 . . . . . .900.00 – 1,200.00

Row 3:

      Old Shoe, 1959, W23 . . . . . . . . . . . . . . . . .90.00 – 130.00
      Humpty Dumpty with peaked hat, 1962,
      W29 . . . . . . . . . . . . . . . . . . . . . . . . . . . . . .175.00 – 250.00

---

This drawing was submitted, but for some reason the cookie jar was never produced.

Row 1:
      Red Riding Hood, 1956, K24D . . . . . . . . .$550.00 – 650.00

      Raggedy Ann, 1956, W16 . . . . . . . . . . . . . .300.00 – 350.00

Row 2:
      Antique Touring Car, 1971, W53 . . . . . . . .minimum 800.00

      Fish, 1971, W52 . . . . . . . . . . . . . . . . . . . .400.00 – 500.00

Row 3:
      Davy Crockett, 1956 . . . . . . . . . . . . . . . . .175.00 – 300.00

      Matching Mug . . . . . . . . . . . . . . . . . . . . . . .35.00 – 75.00

      Peter Pan, 1956, K23D . . . . . . . . . . . . . . . .600.00 – 800.00

Row 1:

        Little Angel, 1956, W17 . . . . . . . . . . . . . . .$700.00 – 950.00

        Boy with Balloons, 1971, W56 . . . . . . . . . .650.00 – 750.00

Row 2:

        Cow with Cat Finial, purple glaze – W50,

        1970 . . . . . . . . . . . . . . . . . . . . . . . . . . .minimum 1,000.00

        White Hen on Basket, 1969, W44 . . . . . . . . . .65.00 – 95.00

Row 3:

        Clown, Bust, 1970, W49 . . . . . . . . . . . . . . .250.00 – 350.00

        Cookie House, white with pastels – 1965,

        W31 . . . . . . . . . . . . . . . . . . . . . . . . . . . . . .65.00 – 95.00

        In older glaze, 1962 . . . . . . . . . . . . . . . . . . .85.00 – 125.00

Row 1:

        Hobby Horse, 1971, W55 . . . . . . . . . . . . . .$450.00 – 550.00

Row 2:

        Humpty Dumpty with Beanie and Bow Tie,
        1956 – 1961, W18 . . . . . . . . . . . . . . . . . . . .250.00 – 300.00
        Pumpkin Cookie Jar, 1959 – 61, W24 . . . . .250.00 – 300.00

Row 3:

        Stylized Siamese, 1967, W41 . . . . . . . . . . .350.00 – 400.00
        Stylized Owl, 1967, W42 . . . . . . . . . . . . . .175.00 – 250.00

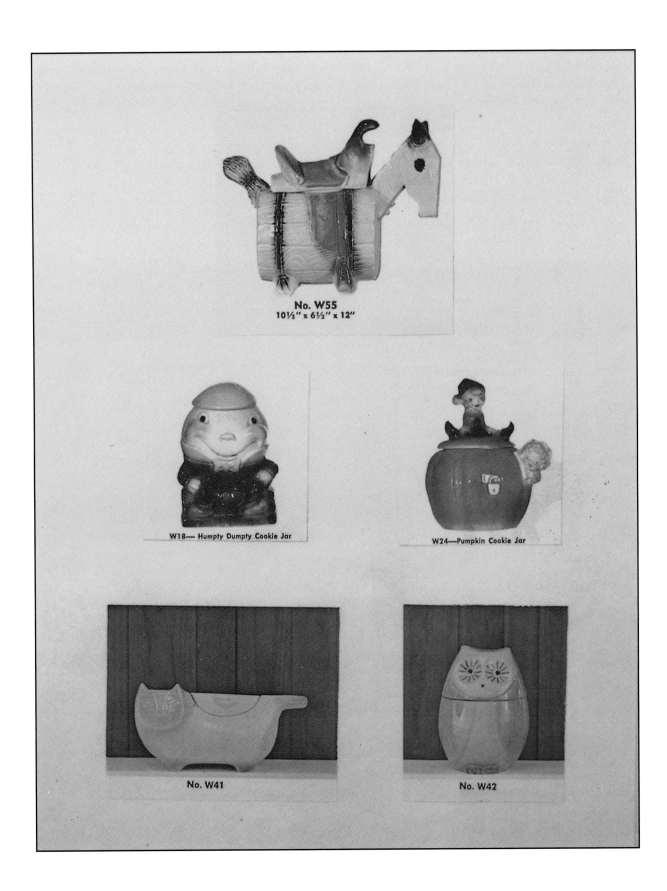

**No. W55**
10½" x 6½" x 12"

W18— Humpty Dumpty Cookie Jar

W24—Pumpkin Cookie Jar

No. W41

No. W42

Row 1:

Puppy Police, 1966, W39 . . . . . . . . . . . . . .$500.00 – 600.00
Chick and Nest, 1966, W38 . . . . . . . . . . . .250.00 – 300.00
Sitting Piggy, 1966, W37 . . . . . . . . . . . . . .400.00 – 450.00

Row 2:

Teddy Bear, feet apart, early 1950s, W14 . . .225.00 – 275.00
Squirrel in Top Hat, early 1950s, W15 . . . . .225.00 – 300.00

Row 3:

Dog with Basket, 1971, W54 . . . . . . . . . . .250.00 – 300.00
Treasure Chest, 1962, W28 . . . . . . . . . . . . .100.00 – 150.00
Covered Wagon, 1962, W30 . . . . . . . . . . . .550.00 – 650.00

W39—Puppy Police Cookie Jar

W38—Chick & Nest Cookie Jar

W37—Sitting Piggy Cookie Jar

W14—Teddy Bear Cookie Jar

W15—Squirrel Cookie Jar

No. W54
8" x 12½" x 6½"

W28—Treasure Chest Cookie Jar

W30—Covered Wagon Cookie Jar

Row 1:

        Little Boy Blue, 1956, K25D . . . . . . . . . .$650.00 – 750.00
        Matching Mug . . . . . . . . . . . . . . . . . . . . . . . .40.00 – 75.00
        Clown, yellow pants – 1964, W22 . . . . . . . .150.00 – 185.00

Row 2:

        Donkey and Cart, ears down, 1965, W33 . . .350.00 – 400.00
        Donkey and Cart, ears up, 1964, W33 . . . .800.00 – 1,000.00

Row 3:

        Sitting Hippo, 1969, W45 . . . . . . . . . . . . . .250.00 – 350.00
        Laughing Hippo, 1961, W27 . . . . . . . . . . . .450.00 – 550.00
        Smiling Bear, 1969, W46 . . . . . . . . . . . . . .250.00 – 350.00

Cookie Jar
K25D

Mug
K250D

LITTLE BOY BLUE

W22—Clown Cookie Jar

W33—Donkey & Cart Cookie Jar

No. W45
7"x7"x10¾"

W27—Laughing Hippo Cookie Jar

No. W46
7"x7½"x11"

Row 1:

      Circus Horse, early 1950s, W9 . . . . . . . .$750.00 – 1,000.00

      Elephant, wearing baby hat, early 1950s,

      W8 . . . . . . . . . . . . . . . . . . . . . . . . . . . . .350.00 – 450.00

Row 2:

      Little Girl, 1957, W17 . . . . . . . . . . . . . . . . .500.00 – 600.00

      Granny, polka dots on skirt – 1957, W19 . . .300.00 – 350.00

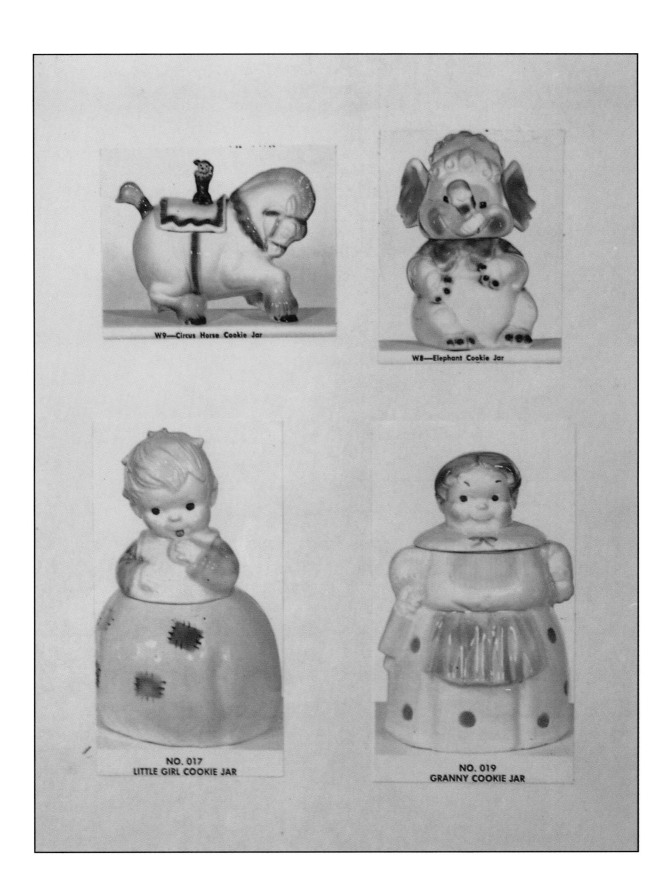

W9—Circus Horse Cookie Jar

W8—Elephant Cookie Jar

NO. 017
LITTLE GIRL COOKIE JAR

NO. 019
GRANNY COOKIE JAR

Row 1:

        Doghouse Wall Pocket, 1952 . . . . . . . . . . . .$75.00 – 100.00

Row 2:

        Horse Wall Pocket, Shape #545,
        USA, 1956 . . . . . . . . . . . . . . . . . . . . . . . . .75.00 – 115.00
        Boxer Wall Pocket, Shape #542,
        USA, 1956 . . . . . . . . . . . . . . . . . . . . . . . . .100.00 – 150.00

Row 3:

        Horse Wall Pocket, 1952 . . . . . . . . . . . . . . . .75.00 – 115.00

Row 4:

        Fish Wall Pocket, 1958 . . . . . . . . . . . . . . . . . .65.00 – 95.00
        Duck Wall Pocket, 1956 . . . . . . . . . . . . . . . . .65.00 – 95.00

Row 1:

      Wall Plaque, 1950s . . . . . . . . . . . . . . . . . . . . .$50.00 – 75.00

Row 2:

      Ivotint Wall Pocket, 6", 1928 . . . . . . . . . . . . .85.00 – 140.00
      Mermaid Bathroom Jewelry Caddy, 1954 . . .75.00 – 150.00
      Cactus Wall Pocket, 1928 . . . . . . . . . . . . . . . .65.00 – 95.00

Row 3:

      Blended Roman Wall Pocket, 6",
      Shape #455, 1927 . . . . . . . . . . . . . . . . . . . . .75.00 – 150.00

Row 4:

      African Masks Wall Plaques, 10½", USA,
      1958 . . . . . . . . . . . . . . . . . . . . . . . . . . . . .75.00 – 150.00 pr.

Row 1:
    Rooster Planter, 1956 . . . . . . . . . . . . . . . . . . .$25.00 – 40.00
    Twin Swans Planter, USA, 1941 . . . . . . . . . . . .35.00 – 45.00

Row 2:
    Ostrich Planter, Brush 109, 1950s . . . . . . . . . .25.00 – 40.00
    Swan Planter, Brush USA 681, 1956 . . . . . . . .30.00 – 40.00
    Duck Planter, 560, 1952 . . . . . . . . . . . . . . . . .20.00 – 30.00

Row 3:
    Duck Planter, USA 133, 1950s . . . . . . . . . . . .35.00 – 45.00
    Swan Planter, Brush USA 629 . . . . . . . . . . . .30.00 – 50.00

Row 4:
    Rooster Ornament, 1956 . . . . . . . . . . . . . . .200.00 – 300.00
    Swan Planter, USA, 1950s . . . . . . . . . . . . . .25.00 – 35.00
    Chicken Ornament, 1956 . . . . . . . . . . . . . .150.00 – 250.00

**Row 1:**

Bear, 1941 . . . . . . . . . . . . . . . . . . . . . . . . . . . . .$15.00 – 20.00
Goat, 1952 . . . . . . . . . . . . . . . . . . . . . . . . . . . .15.00 – 20.00
Camel, 1950s . . . . . . . . . . . . . . . . . . . . . . . . . .20.00 – 30.00

**Row 2:**

Frog, Gold and Black paper label, 1930s . . . . .35.00 – 45.00
Trojan Horse, 1939 . . . . . . . . . . . . . . . . . . . . .25.00 – 35.00
Pig Bank, 1956 . . . . . . . . . . . . . . . . . . . . . . . .35.00 – 45.00

**Row 3:**

Chicken, late 1930s . . . . . . . . . . . . . . . . . . . . .15.00 – 20.00
Elephant, late 1930s . . . . . . . . . . . . . . . . . . . .25.00 – 35.00
Swan, late 1930s . . . . . . . . . . . . . . . . . . . . . . .20.00 – 25.00

**Row 4:**

Deer, late 1930s . . . . . . . . . . . . . . . . . . . . . . . .15.00 – 20.00
Horse, late 1930s . . . . . . . . . . . . . . . . . . . . . . .30.00 – 35.00
Puppy, late 1930s . . . . . . . . . . . . . . . . . . . . . . .15.00 – 20.00

**Row 5:**

Hobby Horse, 1950s . . . . . . . . . . . . . . . . . . . . .20.00 – 25.00
Kitten with Shoe, 1958 . . . . . . . . . . . . . . . . . .15.00 – 20.00
Skunk and Cart, 1958 . . . . . . . . . . . . . . . . . . .15.00 – 20.00

**Row 6:**

Fish, 1939 . . . . . . . . . . . . . . . . . . . . . . . . . . . . .25.00 – 40.00
Girl and Hobby Horse, 1950s . . . . . . . . . . . . .15.00 – 20.00
Lamb, 1950s . . . . . . . . . . . . . . . . . . . . . . . . . . .10.00 – 20.00

Row 1:

       Donkey and Stump, gold paper label, 1956 . .$15.00 – 20.00

       Flowerpot, 1950s . . . . . . . . . . . . . . . . . . . . . . .10.00 – 15.00

       Lamb and Corral, 1950s . . . . . . . . . . . . . . . . .12.00 – 15.00

Row 2:

       Puppy Planter, 1956 . . . . . . . . . . . . . . . . . . . . .15.00 – 20.00

       Cat and Bucket, 1956 . . . . . . . . . . . . . . . . . . .15.00 – 20.00

       Dog and Stump, 1950s . . . . . . . . . . . . . . . . . .12.00 – 15.00

Row 3:

       Bird Planter, USA #246, 1957 . . . . . . . . . . . . .20.00 – 25.00

       Elephant, 1939 . . . . . . . . . . . . . . . . . . . . . . . . .5.00 – 15.00

       Bird Planter, 1957 . . . . . . . . . . . . . . . . . . . . . .20.00 – 25.00

Row 4:

       Birds Planter, 1957 . . . . . . . . . . . . . . . . . . . . .30.00 – 50.00

       Puppies Planter, 1957 . . . . . . . . . . . . . . . . . . .30.00 – 50.00

       Bear on Log, 1957 . . . . . . . . . . . . . . . . . . . . . .30.00 – 50.00

Row 5:

       Raccoon on Log, 1957 . . . . . . . . . . . . . . . . . . .30.00 – 50.00

       Squirrel on Log, 1957 . . . . . . . . . . . . . . . . . . .30.00 – 50.00

       Rabbit on Log, 1957 . . . . . . . . . . . . . . . . . . . .30.00 – 50.00

Row 6:

       Cat Planter, 1952 . . . . . . . . . . . . . . . . . . . . . . .40.00 – 60.00

       Frog . . . . . . . . . . . . . . . . . . . . . . . . . . . . . . . .12.00 – 20.00

       Elephant, 1939 . . . . . . . . . . . . . . . . . . . . . . . .20.00 – 40.00

Row 1:

        Duck, 1941 . . . . . . . . . . . . . . . . . . . . . . . . . . .$10.00 – 15.00

        Duckling, 1941 . . . . . . . . . . . . . . . . . . . . . . .10.00 – 15.00

        Pig, 1952 . . . . . . . . . . . . . . . . . . . . . . . . . . . . .8.00 – 10.00

        Duck, 1941 . . . . . . . . . . . . . . . . . . . . . . . . . . .8.00 – 15.00

Row 2:

        Cowboy Planter, 1940s . . . . . . . . . . . . . . . . . .20.00 – 35.00

        Madonna, 1941 . . . . . . . . . . . . . . . . . . . . . . . .10.00 – 20.00

        Bird Planter, 1930s . . . . . . . . . . . . . . . . . . . . .12.00 – 20.00

        Mermaid Planter, USA, #245, 1940s . . . . . . . .25.00 – 45.00

Row 3:

        Deer Planter, 1940s . . . . . . . . . . . . . . . . . . . . .10.00 – 15.00

        Hand-Painted Cat, 1940s . . . . . . . . . . . . . . . . .15.00 – 25.00

        Camel, 1940s . . . . . . . . . . . . . . . . . . . . . . . . . .10.00 – 20.00

        Deer, 1940s . . . . . . . . . . . . . . . . . . . . . . . . . . .10.00 – 20.00

Row 4:

        Deer Planter, 1950s . . . . . . . . . . . . . . . . . . . . .12.00 – 15.00

        Turtle Planter, USA, #205, 1940s . . . . . . . . . .25.00 – 35.00

        Deer, 1940s . . . . . . . . . . . . . . . . . . . . . . . . . . .20.00 – 25.00

        Deer, 1950s . . . . . . . . . . . . . . . . . . . . . . . . . . .15.00 – 20.00

Row 5:

        Rabbit . . . . . . . . . . . . . . . . . . . . . . . . . . . . . . .10.00 – 20.00

        Rabbit, removable carrot . . . . . . . . . . . . . . . . .45.00 – 65.00

        Rabbit Planter, 1940 . . . . . . . . . . . . . . . . . . . . .10.00 – 20.00

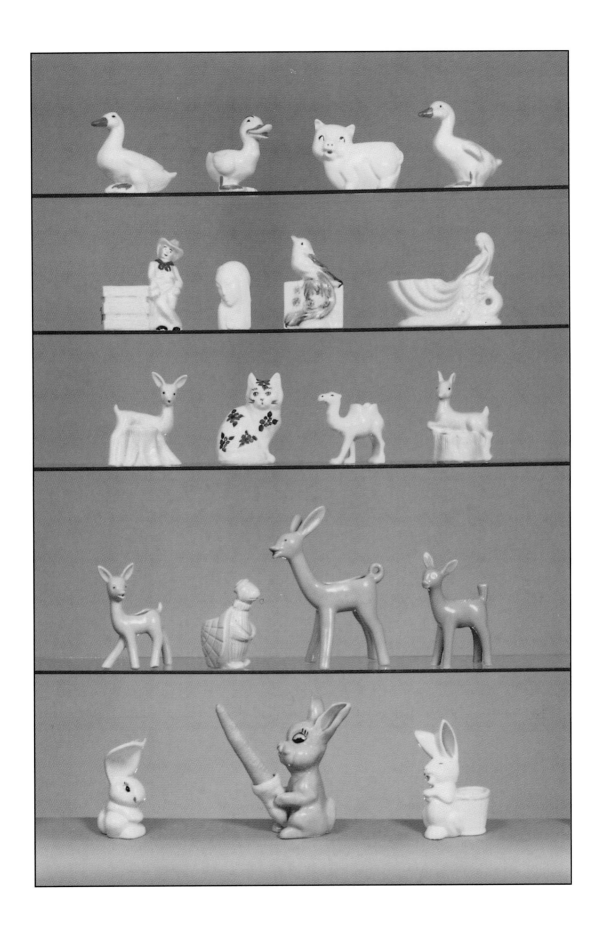

Row 1:

      Miniature Vases and Planters, 1939 . . . . . . .$8.00 – 15.00 ea.

Row 2:

      Elephant, 1939 . . . . . . . . . . . . . . . . . . . . . . . . .8.00 – 15.00
      Miniature Vase, 1939 . . . . . . . . . . . . . . . . . . . .8.00 – 10.00
      Double Shoe Planter, 1971 . . . . . . . . . . . . . . . .8.00 – 20.00
      Baby Shoe, 1939 . . . . . . . . . . . . . . . . . . . . . . . .8.00 – 10.00
      Boot, 1939 . . . . . . . . . . . . . . . . . . . . . . . . . . . . .8.00 – 10.00
      Miniature Vase, 1939 . . . . . . . . . . . . . . . . . . . .8.00 – 15.00

Row 3:

      Miniature Animals, 1939 – 40 . . . . . . . . . . .10.00 – 20.00 ea.
      Harlequin animal collectors note gold duck!

Row 4:

      Dog, 1940s . . . . . . . . . . . . . . . . . . . . . . . . . .20.00 – 25.00
      Penguin, 1940s . . . . . . . . . . . . . . . . . . . . . . .15.00 – 25.00
      Rabbit Planter, 1940s . . . . . . . . . . . . . . . . . .15.00 – 20.00
      Dog, 1939 . . . . . . . . . . . . . . . . . . . . . . . . . . .20.00 – 25.00

Row 5:

      Dog, 1939 . . . . . . . . . . . . . . . . . . . . . . . . . . .15.00 – 20.00
      Dog, 1940s . . . . . . . . . . . . . . . . . . . . . . . . . .20.00 – 25.00
      Puppy, 1952 . . . . . . . . . . . . . . . . . . . . . . . . . .10.00 – 15.00
      Puppy, 1952 . . . . . . . . . . . . . . . . . . . . . . . . . .10.00 – 15.00

Row 6:

      Cow, 1940s . . . . . . . . . . . . . . . . . . . . . . . . . .20.00 – 30.00
      Cow with Calf, 1940s . . . . . . . . . . . . . . . . . .25.00 – 35.00
      Bull, 1941 (Ferdinand) . . . . . . . . . . . . . . . . .30.00 – 45.00

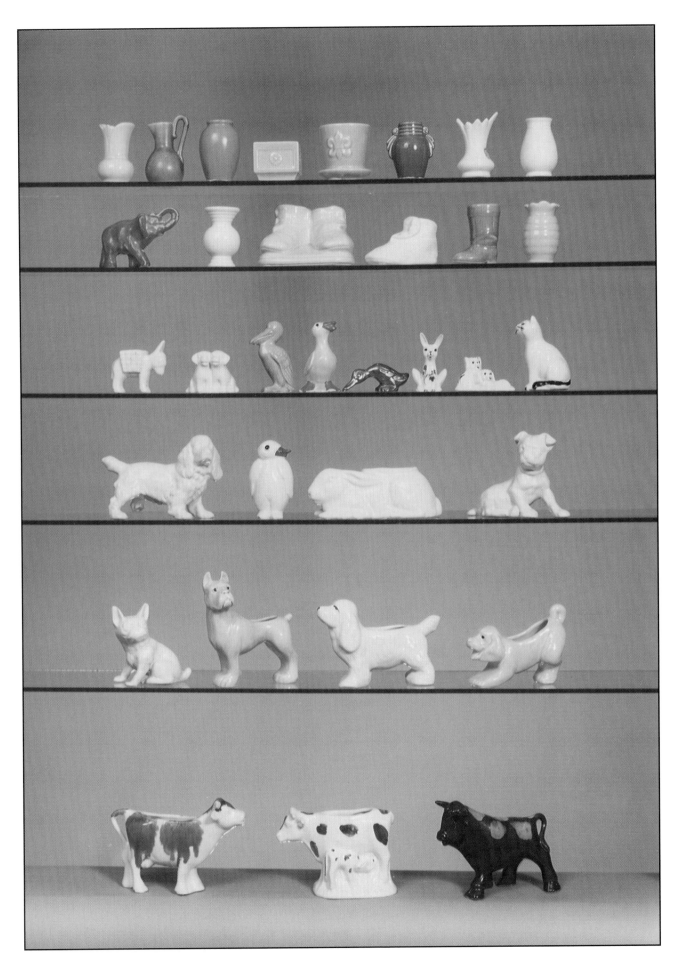

Row 1:

        Locomotive, 1956 . . . . . . . . . . . . . . . . . . . . . .$15.00 – 25.00

        Steamboat, 1956 . . . . . . . . . . . . . . . . . . . . .10.00 – 20.00

        Old Car, 1956 . . . . . . . . . . . . . . . . . . . . . . . .10.00 – 20.00

Row 2:

        Double Pipe Planter, 1950s . . . . . . . . . . . . . . .10.00 – 20.00

        Covered Wagon . . . . . . . . . . . . . . . . . . . . . . .10.00 – 15.00

        Conch, 1955 . . . . . . . . . . . . . . . . . . . . . . . . .15.00 – 20.00

        Pirate, 1950s . . . . . . . . . . . . . . . . . . . . . . . . .10.00 – 15.00

Row 3:

        Sailboat Ornament, 1950s . . . . . . . . . . . . . . . .45.00 – 75.00

        Locomotive Planter, 1956 . . . . . . . . . . . . . . . .30.00 – 65.00

Row 4:

        Car Planter, 1950s . . . . . . . . . . . . . . . . . . . . . .20.00 – 45.00

        Boat Planter, 1958 . . . . . . . . . . . . . . . . . . . . . .20.00 – 40.00

Row 5:

        Horse and Carriage Planter, 1958 . . . . . . . . . . .25.00 – 45.00

        House Planter, USA, #887 . . . . . . . . . . . . . . . .25.00 – 45.00

Row 6:

        Sea Gull Planter, 1956 . . . . . . . . . . . . . . . . . . .25.00 – 45.00

        Mare with Foal Planter, 1958 . . . . . . . . . . . . . .25.00 – 45.00

Row 1:

Vase, 6", USA, #502 . . . . . . . . . . . . . . . . . . . . . .$15.00 – 25.00
Basket, 1939 . . . . . . . . . . . . . . . . . . . . . . . . .75.00 – 100.00
Vase, 6", 1940s . . . . . . . . . . . . . . . . . . . . . . . .15.00 – 25.00

Row 2:

Vase, 7", 1962 . . . . . . . . . . . . . . . . . . . . . . . . .10.00 – 15.00
Dutch Shoes, hand painted, 1940 . . . . . . . .15.00 – 25.00 ea.
Vase, 6", #579, 1939 . . . . . . . . . . . . . . . . . . . . .10.00 – 20.00

Row 3:

Carriage Planter, 1956 . . . . . . . . . . . . . . . . . . .12.00 – 20.00
Carriage Planter, 1971 . . . . . . . . . . . . . . . . . . .10.00 – 15.00
Carriage Planter, USA, 1956 . . . . . . . . . . . . . .10.00 – 15.00

Row 4:

Little Bo Peep, 1941 . . . . . . . . . . . . . . . . . . . .20.00 – 40.00
Southern Lady, 1941 . . . . . . . . . . . . . . . . . . . .25.00 – 40.00
Basket Girl, smaller of two sizes, 1941 . . . . . .30.00 – 50.00

Row 5:

Girl with Hoop Skirt, 1941 . . . . . . . . . . . . . . .20.00 – 35.00
Red Riding Hood, Brush USA, 1941 . . . . . . . .30.00 – 50.00
Madonna . . . . . . . . . . . . . . . . . . . . . . . . . . . . .15.00 – 25.00

Row 1:

       Jardiniere with Removable Pot, Pallette #692,
       1952 . . . . . . . . . . . . . . . . . . . . . . . . . . . . . . . . . . . . .$10.00 – 15.00
       Bowl, #353, 1950s . . . . . . . . . . . . . . . . . . . . .15.00 – 20.00
       Planter, 1950s . . . . . . . . . . . . . . . . . . . . . . . . .10.00 – 15.00

Row 2:

       Cactus Planter with Removable Pots, 1950s . . .25.00 – 30.00
       Flowerpot, 1950s . . . . . . . . . . . . . . . . . . . . . .10.00 – 15.00
       Acorn and Oak Leaf Planter with
       Removable Pots . . . . . . . . . . . . . . . . . . . . . . . .25.00 – 30.00

Row 3:

       Miniature Vases, 1939 . . . . . . . . . . . . . . . . .10.00 – 20.00 ea.
       Planter with Tulip, Brush USA, 1950s . . . . . . .20.00 – 25.00

Row 4:

       Miniature Vases, 1939 . . . . . . . . . . . . . . . . .10.00 – 20.00 ea.
       Planter with Removable Pots, 1952 . . . . . . . .30.00 – 45.00

Row 5:

       Miniature Vases, 1939 . . . . . . . . . . . . . . . . .10.00 – 20.00 ea.
       Planter with Floral Motif, USA #40A, 1939 . . .25.00 – 30.00

# BITTERSWEET, 1945

Row 1:
>  Double Cornucopia Planter, 4½" .........$45.00 – 75.00

Row 2:
>  Pedestal Planter, 7" .....................50.00 – 80.00
>  Bud Vase, 6½" .........................30.00 – 40.00
>  Flowerpot, 6½" ........................20.00 – 30.00

Row 3:
>  Vase, 8" ..............................30.00 – 50.00
>  Bowl, 4½", Black and Gold paper label ......25.00 – 35.00
>  Vase, 10" .............................35.00 – 50.00

Row 4:
>  Vase, 6" ..............................20.00 – 30.00
>  Vase, 10" .............................65.00 – 95.00
>  Cornucopia, 4" ........................40.00 – 45.00

# PRINCESS, MID-1960s

Row 1:
    Footed Planter, 3" x 13½" . . . . . . . . . . . . . . . .$35.00 – 45.00

Row 2:
    Planter, 3" x 7" . . . . . . . . . . . . . . . . . . . . . . .15.00 – 20.00
    Planter, 3½" x 12½" . . . . . . . . . . . . . . . . . . .25.00 – 35.00

Row 3:
    Planter, 3" x 10½" . . . . . . . . . . . . . . . . . . . .25.00 – 35.00
    Planter, 3" x 8" . . . . . . . . . . . . . . . . . . . . . . .15.00 – 20.00

Row 4:
    Planter, 3" x 8" . . . . . . . . . . . . . . . . . . . . . . .15.00 – 20.00
    Footed Vase, 5" . . . . . . . . . . . . . . . . . . . . . . .20.00 – 25.00
    Footed Planter, 3½" x 8½" . . . . . . . . . . . . . . .20.00 – 25.00

Row 5:
    Vase, 7" . . . . . . . . . . . . . . . . . . . . . . . . . . . .25.00 – 35.00
    Vase, 12" . . . . . . . . . . . . . . . . . . . . . . . . . . .50.00 – 75.00
    Vase, 5" . . . . . . . . . . . . . . . . . . . . . . . . . . . .20.00 – 25.00

# UNNAMED LINE, LATE 1940s – EARLY 1950s

Row 1:
      Vase, 8" . . . . . . . . . . . . . . . . . . . . . . . . . . . . .$20.00 – 30.00
      Vase, 9" . . . . . . . . . . . . . . . . . . . . . . . . . . . . .25.00 – 35.00

Row 2:
      Vase, 8", USA #220 . . . . . . . . . . . . . . . . . . . . .25.00 – 40.00
      Planter, 8½", USA #221 . . . . . . . . . . . . . . . .20.00 – 30.00
      Vase, 9" . . . . . . . . . . . . . . . . . . . . . . . . . . . . .35.00 – 45.00

Row 3:
      Vase, 10" . . . . . . . . . . . . . . . . . . . . . . . . . . . .35.00 – 45.00
      Vase, USA #500 . . . . . . . . . . . . . . . . . . . . . . .40.00 – 50.00
      Vase, 10" . . . . . . . . . . . . . . . . . . . . . . . . . . . .30.00 – 40.00

Row 4:
      Vase, 12", USA #843 . . . . . . . . . . . . . . . . . . . .45.00 – 60.00
      Vase, 12" . . . . . . . . . . . . . . . . . . . . . . . . . . . .40.00 – 50.00

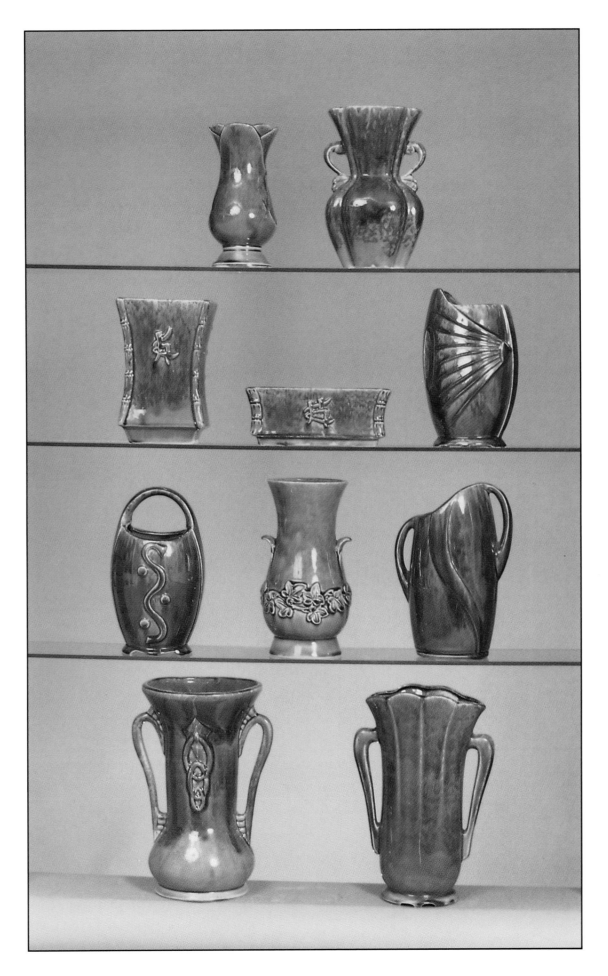

# BRONZE LINE, 1956

Row 1:

      Carafe, 9", Palette mark #928 . . . . . . . . . . . . .$40.00 – 50.00

      Footed Bowl, 9½" x 4½" . . . . . . . . . . . . . . . .25.00 – 35.00

Row 2:

      Bud Vase, 7½" . . . . . . . . . . . . . . . . . . . . . . . .20.00 – 30.00

      Footed Bowl, 11½" x 4½", USA . . . . . . . . . . .25.00 – 35.00

Row 3:

      Vase, 10½" . . . . . . . . . . . . . . . . . . . . . . . . . . .35.00 – 45.00

      Flower Arranger with Candlestick,

      Palette mark . . . . . . . . . . . . . . . . . . . . . . . . . .35.00 – 45.00

      Vase, 7", Palette mark . . . . . . . . . . . . . . . . . .30.00 – 40.00

Row 4:

      Pedestal Bowl, 5", Palette mark . . . . . . . . . . .20.00 – 30.00

      Vase, 10" . . . . . . . . . . . . . . . . . . . . . . . . . . . .35.00 – 45.00

      Vase, 8", Palette, USA #720 . . . . . . . . . . . . . .30.00 – 40.00

Row 1:

  Planter, 3", 1952 . . . . . . . . . . . . . . . . . . . . . . .$10.00 – 15.00

  Vase, 8", USA #220, 1952 . . . . . . . . . . . . . . . .25.00 – 35.00

  Planter, 4", #222, 1950s . . . . . . . . . . . . . . . .10.00 – 15.00

Row 2:

  Vase, 8", 1950s . . . . . . . . . . . . . . . . . . . . . . .25.00 – 35.00

  Pillow Vase, 6" . . . . . . . . . . . . . . . . . . . . . . .20.00 – 30.00

  Pillow Vase, 8" . . . . . . . . . . . . . . . . . . . . . . .30.00 – 40.00

Row 3:

  Flowerpot, 4" . . . . . . . . . . . . . . . . . . . . . . . .10.00 – 15.00

  Planter, 9" x 3½" . . . . . . . . . . . . . . . . . . . . . .25.00 – 30.00

  Jardiniere, 4" . . . . . . . . . . . . . . . . . . . . . . . .10.00 – 15.00

Row 4:

  Vase, Oriental motif, 7½", USA #225 . . . . . . . .25.00 – 35.00

  Flowerpot, 5½", USA #853, 1950s . . . . . . . . .10.00 – 15.00

  Vase, 8", USA #856, 1950s . . . . . . . . . . . . . .20.00 – 30.00

Row 5:

  Jardiniere, 3½" . . . . . . . . . . . . . . . . . . . . . . .10.00 – 15.00

  Vase, 10" . . . . . . . . . . . . . . . . . . . . . . . . . . .35.00 – 45.00

  Pillow Vase, 5" x 6", #13, 1950s . . . . . . . . . . .10.00 – 15.00

151

Row 1:

       Ewer, 7", 1950s . . . . . . . . . . . . . . . . . . . . . . . .$15.00 – 25.00

       Pitcher, 7½", early 1940s . . . . . . . . . . . . . . . .35.00 – 45.00

       Ewer, 7", Brush USA . . . . . . . . . . . . . . . . . . . .20.00 – 30.00

Row 2:

       Vase, 9", Palette mark #719 . . . . . . . . . . . . . .25.00 – 35.00

       Pitcher Vase, 10½", early 1940s . . . . . . . . . . .20.00 – 30.00

       Vase, 9½", USA #214, 1940s . . . . . . . . . . . . .20.00 – 30.00

Row 3:

       Vase, 8", USA #074, mid-1950s . . . . . . . . . . .20.00 – 30.00

       Vase, 10", USA, mid-1950s . . . . . . . . . . . . . .25.00 – 35.00

       Vase, 8", USA #075, mid-1950s . . . . . . . . . . .20.00 – 30.00

Row 4:

       Moderne Vase, 7½", early 1930s . . . . . . . . . . .35.00 – 50.00

       Rose Jar, 11", early 1930s . . . . . . . . . . . . . . .85.00 – 125.00

       Rose Jar, 7½", early 1930s . . . . . . . . . . . . . . .65.00 – 95.00

Assorted cobweb vases, $30.00 – 45.00.

Row 1:

        Footed Planter, 4½", Brush USA, 1941 . . . . .$25.00 – 35.00

        Vase, Nymph Shape, 10", early 1930s . . . . . . .40.00 – 50.00

        Planter, 5", #71HR Brush USA, 1962 . . . . . . . .15.00 – 25.00

Row 2:

        Pedestal Planter, 4", #927 Brush USA, 1957 . .10.00 – 15.00

        Basket, 9½", USA #658 . . . . . . . . . . . . . . . .50.00 – 75.00

        Pedestal Planter, 5", Palette mark #715, USA .15.00 – 25.00

Row 3:

        Bowl Vase, 6", 1942 . . . . . . . . . . . . . . . . . . . .30.00 – 40.00

        Vase, 7", 1939 . . . . . . . . . . . . . . . . . . . . . . . .75.00 – 100.00

        Vase, 6", 1940s . . . . . . . . . . . . . . . . . . . . . . . .35.00 – 45.00

Row 4:

        Vase, 7", Palette mark #701 USA, 1957 . . . . . .20.00 – 30.00

        Vase, 9", 1961 . . . . . . . . . . . . . . . . . . . . . . . .20.00 – 30.00

        Pitcher Vase, 8", Black and Gold paper label . .20.00 – 30.00

Row 1:

       Vase, 6", 1940s . . . . . . . . . . . . . . . . . . . . . .$25.00 – 35.00

       Vase, 7½", 1939 . . . . . . . . . . . . . . . . . . . . . . .35.00 – 50.00

       Vase, 6½", 1939 . . . . . . . . . . . . . . . . . . . . . . .25.00 – 35.00

Row 2:

       Hanging Basket, 4", 1940 . . . . . . . . . . . . . . . .25.00 – 35.00

       Vase, 7", 1940s . . . . . . . . . . . . . . . . . . . . . . .30.00 – 40.00

       Vase, 7½", mid-1950s . . . . . . . . . . . . . . . . . .20.00 – 30.00

       Vase, 3", 1940 . . . . . . . . . . . . . . . . . . . . . . . .15.00 – 25.00

Row 3:

       Nymph Vase, 10", #520 Brush USA, 1933 . . . .40.00 – 50.00

       Jardiniere, 6½", #292 Brush USA, 1941 . . . . . .25.00 – 35.00

       Vase, 10", 1957 . . . . . . . . . . . . . . . . . . . . . . .35.00 – 45.00

Row 4:

       Vase, 12", 1940 . . . . . . . . . . . . . . . . . . . . . . .75.00 – 100.00

       Vase, 10", 1952 . . . . . . . . . . . . . . . . . . . . . . .45.00 – 60.00

       Tankard 12", #609 Brush USA, 1941 . . . . . . . .65.00 – 80.00

Top:

        Stardust Flying Saucer, 1957 . . . . . . . . . . . .$75.00 – 100.00

Row 1:

        Cactus Hanging Basket, 6", 1928 . . . . . . . . . . .45.00 – 55.00
        Stardust Vase, 8", #601 USA, 1957 . . . . . . . . .50.00 – 75.00
        Cactus Jardiniere, 4", 1928 . . . . . . . . . . . . . .25.00 – 35.00

Row 2:

        *Stardust Hanging Basket, 4", 1957 . . . . . . . .75.00 – 100.00
        Stardust Window Box, 12" x 4", 1957 . . . . . . .55.00 – 95.00
        *Wall Pocket, late 1950s
        Note: This shape was also included in the Stardust line; the tip of
the wall pocket curls up to allow a hanging pot to be hung from it —
both of the Stardust hanging pots on this page were sold with it in the
catalog.
        *These two pieces go together as a hanging basket and hanger.

Row 3:

        Flowerpot, 6", late 1950s . . . . . . . . . . . . . . . .30.00 – 40.00
        Vase, 11½", late 1950s . . . . . . . . . . . . . . . . . .45.00 – 60.00
        Corner Wall Pocket, 6", late 1950s . . . . . . . . . .30.00 – 40.00

Row 1:

        Vase, 8½", 1940 . . . . . . . . . . . . . . . . . . . . . .$15.00 – 30.00

        Vase, 8", early 1930s . . . . . . . . . . . . . . . . . . .30.00 – 40.00

        Vase, 8", Gold paper label, 1957 . . . . . . . . . . .25.00 – 35.00

Row 2:

        Vase, 13½", 1962 . . . . . . . . . . . . . . . . . . . . . . .40.00 – 50.00

        Vase, 12¼", 23K Gold Guaranteed, 1967 . . . . .35.00 – 45.00

        Vase, 12", 1940s . . . . . . . . . . . . . . . . . . . . . . .45.00 – 60.00

Row 3:

        Vase, 12", #546, 1939 . . . . . . . . . . . . . . . . . . .50.00 – 65.00

        Vase, 12", USA #212, late 1940s . . . . . . . . . .50.00 – 75.00

        Vase, 12", Brush USA . . . . . . . . . . . . . . . . . . .45.00 – 60.00

Row 1:

       Gazelle Motif Planter, 13½", W5, USA,
       early 1950s . . . . . . . . . . . . . . . . . . . . . . . . .$20.00 – 30.00

Row 2:

       Pillow Vase, 5", W3USA, early 1950s . . . . . . .10.00 – 20.00
       Planter, 10½", W4USA . . . . . . . . . . . . . . . . .15.00 – 25.00
       Planter, 4½", W1USA . . . . . . . . . . . . . . . . . .10.00 – 15.00

Row 3:

       Vase with Wheat Motif, 10", 1939 . . . . . . . . .40.00 – 55.00
       Vase, 10½", #771 . . . . . . . . . . . . . . . . . . . . . .20.00 – 25.00
       Vase, 10½", #503 USA . . . . . . . . . . . . . . . . . .30.00 – 50.00
       Vase, 8", #543 USA, early 1940s . . . . . . . . . .30.00 – 45.00

Row 4:

       Vase, 9", 1939 . . . . . . . . . . . . . . . . . . . . . . . .20.00 – 40.00
       Vase, 8", 1940s . . . . . . . . . . . . . . . . . . . . . . .15.00 – 25.00
       Vase, 8", 1940 . . . . . . . . . . . . . . . . . . . . . . . .15.00 – 30.00
       Vase, 7", #655, 1939 . . . . . . . . . . . . . . . . . . .10.00 – 25.00

Row 5:

       Cloverleaf Kitchen Accessories, 1955
       Salt and Pepper Shakers . . . . . . . . . . . . . . . .40.00 – 60.00 pr.
       Pitcher, 6½", #K11 USA . . . . . . . . . . . . . . . .45.00 – 75.00
       Cookie Jar, 9", #K13 USA . . . . . . . . . . . . . .95.00 – 115.00
       Sugar Bowl, #K4 . . . . . . . . . . . . . . . . . . . . . .30.00 – 45.00

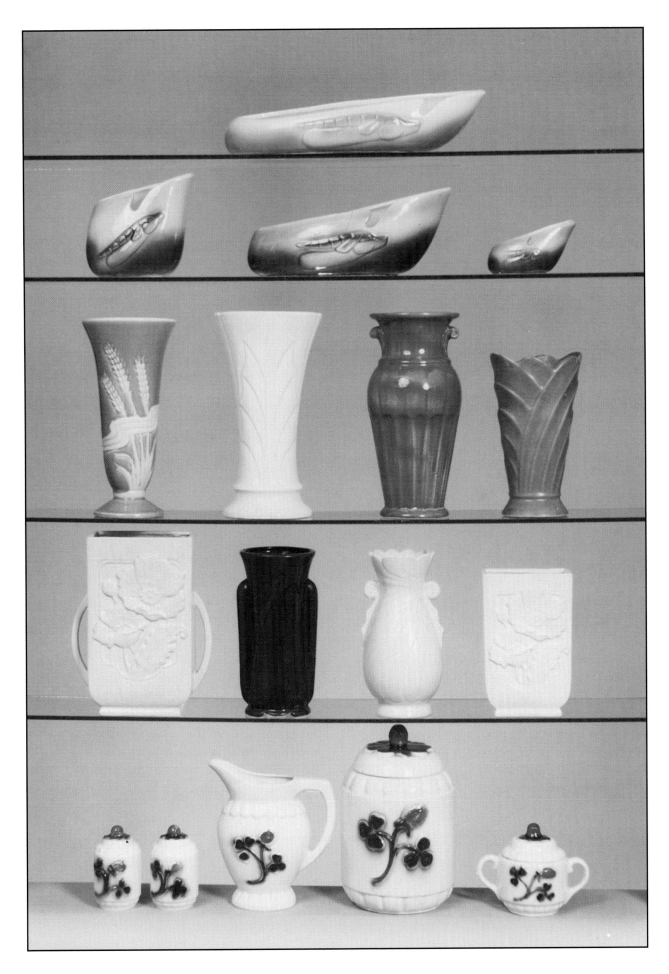

Row 1:

       Bud Vase, 7", #75, early 1940s . . . . . . . . . . .$25.00 – 35.00

       Salada Teapot, 4", Made in USA, mid-1920s . . . .20.00 – 30.00

       Bud Vase, 9½", #510 Brush USA, 1961 . . . . . .20.00 – 35.00

Row 2:

       Jardiniere, 5" . . . . . . . . . . . . . . . . . . . . . . . . . .15.00 – 30.00

       Vase, 7½", mid-1950s . . . . . . . . . . . . . . . . . . .35.00 – 50.00

       Pedestal Bowl, 5", Pallette mark #716, 1947 . .15.00 – 25.00

Row 3:

       Vase, 6" . . . . . . . . . . . . . . . . . . . . . . . . . . . . .20.00 – 25.00

       Cornucopia Vase, 8", 1940 . . . . . . . . . . . . . . .25.00 – 35.00

       Planter, 4½", 1956 . . . . . . . . . . . . . . . . . . . . . .20.00 – 25.00

Row 4:

       Planter, 3" x 10", 1938 . . . . . . . . . . . . . . . . . .15.00 – 20.00

       Planter, 10" x 4", 1938 . . . . . . . . . . . . . . . . . .15.00 – 25.00

Row 5:

       Vase, 5", 24K gold, 1968 . . . . . . . . . . . . . . . . .15.00 – 25.00

       Vase, early 1930s . . . . . . . . . . . . . . . . . . . . . .30.00 – 45.00

       Pitcher Vase, 7", 1950s . . . . . . . . . . . . . . . . . .15.00 – 25.00

Row 1:

        Pitcher, 5½", 1940s . . . . . . . . . . . . . . . . . . . . .$30.00 – 40.00

        Vase, 5" . . . . . . . . . . . . . . . . . . . . . . . . . . . . .25.00 – 30.00

        Pitcher, 5½", early 1930s . . . . . . . . . . . . . . . .25.00 – 35.00

Row 2:

        Pitcher Vase, 7", Brush USA, 1941 . . . . . . . . . .25.00 – 35.00

        "V" Vase, 6", 1939 . . . . . . . . . . . . . . . . . . . . .30.00 – 40.00

        Vase, 7", #708 . . . . . . . . . . . . . . . . . . . . . . . . .20.00 – 30.00

Row 3:

        Vase, 6", 1939 . . . . . . . . . . . . . . . . . . . . . . . . .20.00 – 35.00

        Vase, Southern Belle motif, #218 USA . . . . . . .40.00 – 60.00

        Creamer, 5", #23F USA, 1940s . . . . . . . . . . . .15.00 – 20.00

Row 4:

        Vase, 6" . . . . . . . . . . . . . . . . . . . . . . . . . . . . .10.00 – 15.00

        "V" Vase, 8", early 1940s . . . . . . . . . . . . . . . .50.00 – 80.00

        Pitcher, 6", #561 Brush USA . . . . . . . . . . . . . .15.00 – 25.00

Row 1:

      Vase, 10½", #546, 1939 . . . . . . . . . . . . . . . . . .$20.00 – 35.00

      Vase, 11", #690 USA . . . . . . . . . . . . . . . . . . . .40.00 – 50.00

      Vase, 10", #502, USA . . . . . . . . . . . . . . . . . .35.00 – 45.00

Row 2:

      Vase, 8½", 1939 . . . . . . . . . . . . . . . . . . . . . .20.00 – 35.00

      Vase, 8½", #605 Brush USA, 1940 . . . . . . . . .40.00 – 50.00

      Vase, 7½", 1939 . . . . . . . . . . . . . . . . . . . . . .20.00 – 35.00

Row 3:

      Lamp Base, 12", 1950s . . . . . . . . . . . . . . . . . .25.00 – 35.00

      Vase, 18½", #514, Brush USA, 1954 . . . . . . .75.00 – 100.00

      Vase, 12", USA . . . . . . . . . . . . . . . . . . . . . . .40.00 – 50.00

Row 1:

        Glo Art Vase, 8", #769, 1939 . . . . . . . . . . . .$50.00 – 75.00

        Glo Art Vase, 9", #773, 1939 . . . . . . . . . . . . .55.00 – 85.00

        Vase, 6½", #048 USA . . . . . . . . . . . . . . . . . . .15.00 – 20.00

Row 2:

        Flowerpot, 4", 1935 . . . . . . . . . . . . . . . . . . . . .25.00 – 30.00

        Love Bird Planter, 5", 1941 . . . . . . . . . . . . . .30.00 – 45.00

        Flowerpot, 5½", #151, 1939 . . . . . . . . . . . . . .20.00 – 30.00

Row 3:

        Flowerpot, 5½", #320, 1952 . . . . . . . . . . . . . .20.00 – 25.00

        Jardiniere, 5½", 1939 . . . . . . . . . . . . . . . . . . .20.00 – 30.00

        Flowerpot, 4", #320 USA, 1952 . . . . . . . . . . .15.00 – 20.00

Row 4:

        Rockcraft Planter, 3", 1933 . . . . . . . . . . . . . . .35.00 – 50.00

        Rockcraft Planter, 3½" x 9", 1933 . . . . . . . . .50.00 – 75.00

        Rockcraft Planter, 2½", Gold paper label, 1933 . . .30.00 – 40.00

Row 5:

        Rockcraft Flowerpot, 5½", 1933 . . . . . . . . . . .30.00 – 50.00

        Rockcraft Flowerpot, 8", 1933 . . . . . . . . . . .100.00 – 140.00

        (Older glazes command higher prices, such as "green-rust" in a glaze.)

        Pebblecraft Flowerpot, 4½", 1933 . . . . . . . . .20.00 – 30.00

Glo-Art assortment. Art Vase, 7", $75.00 – 100.00; Vase, 6", Shape #767, $65.00 – 95.00; Vase, 8", $100.00 – 125.00; Green Vase, 7", Shape #768, $50.00 – 65.00; Vase, 5", Shape #756, $40.00 – 60.00; Vase, 6", Shape #761, $45.00 – 65.00; Vase, 3½", Shape #750, $40.00 – 60.00.

# SPECIAL ORDERS

Row 1:

      Pencil Holder . . . . . . . . . . . . . . . . . . . . . . . .$25.00 – 35.00

      String Holder . . . . . . . . . . . . . . . . . . . . . . . . .25.00 – 35.00

      Pencil or Scissors Holder  . . . . . . . . . . . . . . .25.00 – 35.00

      Pencil Holder . . . . . . . . . . . . . . . . . . . . . . . . .25.00 – 35.00

Row 2:

      Lion Pencil Holder  . . . . . . . . . . . . . . . . . . . . .20.00 – 30.00

      Owl Bank  . . . . . . . . . . . . . . . . . . . . . . . . . . . .45.00 – 65.00

      Elephant Pencil Holder . . . . . . . . . . . . . . . . . .30.00 – 45.00

      Lion Bank  . . . . . . . . . . . . . . . . . . . . . . . . . . . .20.00 – 30.00

Row 3:

      Pig Bank, 5½" x 3", also sold in line, 1960s . . .30.00 – 45.00

      Pig Bank, Brush USA #837, 11", 1964 . . . . . . .45.00 – 70.00

      Pig Bank, 7" x 3" . . . . . . . . . . . . . . . . . . . . . . .35.00 – 55.00

Row 4:

      Birdhouse, sold in line, 1956  . . . . . . . . . . . . .50.00 – 75.00

      Birdhouse, sold in line, 1956  . . . . . . . . . . . . .50.00 – 75.00

Row 1:

      Cross, 7", 1969 . . . . . . . . . . . . . . . . . . . . . . .$30.00 – 40.00

      Candleholder, 13" . . . . . . . . . . . . . . . . . . . . .35.00 – 40.00

      Horace Falcon, 7" . . . . . . . . . . . . . . . . . . . .120.00 – 160.00

Row 2:

      Chick, 2¼", for Fanny Farmer . . . . . . . . . . . . .20.00 – 30.00

      Moon Shoe, inscribed: Exact copy, given to us by ILC Industries, Dover, Delaware, MRLF McArthur, Originator and Manufacturer of Moon Landing Suit, H. L. Hayes; after this original moon shoe was modeled, the people from ILC withdrew their permission to allow it to be marketed.

      Cup, 2½", for Fanny Farmer . . . . . . . . . . . . . .20.00 – 30.00

Row 3:

      Brownie Bank, modeled but not decorated
      by Brush . . . . . . . . . . . . . . . . . . . . . . . . . . .40.00 – 60.00

      Duck, Ashtray-Planter, special order, 1966 . . . .30.00 – 50.00

      Little Duck Ashtray, 1966 . . . . . . . . . . . . . . .15.00 – 25.00

      Frog Planter . . . . . . . . . . . . . . . . . . . . . . . . .30.00 – 50.00

Row 4:

      Rabbit Nursery Light, 10" . . . . . . . . . . . . . . . .20.00 – 30.00

      Figural Jug, 7½", Brush USA #88A . . . . . . .150.00 – 200.00

      Christmas Tree Candleholder, special order . . .30.00 – 50.00

      Santa Mug . . . . . . . . . . . . . . . . . . . . . . . . . .15.00 – 20.00

175

Row 1:

       Patio Ashtray, 10" . . . . . . . . . . . . . . . . . . . . . . $50.00 – 65.00

       Fire Hydrant Ornament, 13" . . . . . . . . . . . . . . .45.00 – 70.00

       Patio Lantern, 12½" . . . . . . . . . . . . . . . . . . . .35.00 – 50.00

Row 2:

       Owl Patio Lantern, 9½" . . . . . . . . . . . . . . . . . .40.00 – 60.00

       Owl Patio Lantern, 10" . . . . . . . . . . . . . . . . . .45.00 – 70.00

       Owl Patio Lantern, 8½" . . . . . . . . . . . . . . . . . .40.00 – 50.00

Row 3:

       Siamese Patio Lantern 12½" . . . . . . . . . . . . . . .45.00 – 75.00

       Fireside Cat, 15½", 1960s . . . . . . . . . . . . . . . .55.00 – 80.00

       Fireside Cat, 12½", 1960s . . . . . . . . . . . . . . . .45.00 – 70.00

       Patio Lantern, 12½", 1965 . . . . . . . . . . . . . . . .45.00 – 70.00

# CATALOG REPRINTS OF THE
# BRUSH-McCOY POTTERY CO.

Many of the older and most beautiful pieces of Brush-McCoy pottery that are contained in the catalog reprint pages that follow are not easily found. Because of this, prices can vary widely since they simply do not come up for sale often enough to even suggest a market value. There are items pictured on these pages that serious collectors would not leave behind at any price. Some are so elusive they seem nonexistent. So to put a value on these items is difficult, to say the least. If the piece is one you personally need to complete your collection, obviously the sky is the limit! We have tried to stay within reasonable boundaries and to evaluate them based on the highest price we personally would pay before saying "this is too much to spend." Your opinion may be entirely different. Values are suggested for items in mint condition. Damage, depending on extent and location, may drastically reduce value.

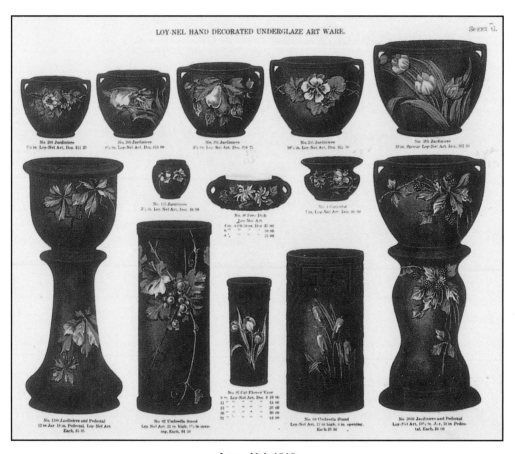

Loy – Nel, 1910

Row 1:
    Jardiniere, 7½" – 12", Shape #205, 5 sizes . . . . . . . . . . . . . .$150.00 – 400.00

Row 2:
    Jardiniere, Shape #115 . . . . . . . . . . . . . . . . . . . . . . . . . . . . . .100.00 – 150.00
    Fern Dish, Shape #90 . . . . . . . . . . . . . . . . . . . . . . . . . . . . . .150.00 – 200.00
    Cuspidor, Shape #1 . . . . . . . . . . . . . . . . . . . . . . . . . . . . . . . .150.00 – 200.00

Row 3:
    Jardiniere and Pedestal, Shape #1180 . . . . . . . . . . . . . . . . . .900.00 – 1,200.00
    Umbrella Stand, 21", Shape #62 . . . . . . . . . . . . . . . . . . . . . .600.00 – 850.00
    Cut Flower Vase, 9" – 21", Shape #97, 5 sizes . . . . . . . . . . . .145.00 – 850.00
    Umbrella Stand, 17", Shape, #60 . . . . . . . . . . . . . . . . . . . . . .550.00 – 800.00
    Jardiniere and Pedestal, Shape #2050 . . . . . . . . . . . . . . . . . .900.00 – 120.00

Blended Glaze

Row 1:

    Umbrella Stand, 17", Shape #64 . . . . . . . . . . . . . . . . . . . . . .$185.00 – 250.00

    Umbrella Stand, 20", Shape #65 . . . . . . . . . . . . . . . . . . . . . . .400.00 – 600.00

    Umbrella Stand, 21", Shape #61 . . . . . . . . . . . . . . . . . . . . . .500.00 – 650.00

    Umbrella Stand, 21", Shape #114 . . . . . . . . . . . . . . . . . . . . .500.00 – 650.00

    Umbrella Stand, 21", Shape #72 . . . . . . . . . . . . . . . . . . . . . .550.00 – 850.00

    Umbrella Stand, 18", Shape #63 . . . . . . . . . . . . . . . . . . . . . .200.00 – 300.00

Row 2:

    Jardiniere and Pedestal, Shape #2140 . . . . . . . . . . . . . . . . . .900.00 – 1,300.00

    Jardiniere and Pedestal, Shape #1130 . . . . . . . . . . . . . . . . . .700.00 – 900.00

    Jardiniere and Pedestal, Shape #2020 . . . . . . . . . . . . . . . . . .300.00 – 500.00

    Jardiniere and Pedestal, Shape #1170 . . . . . . . . . . . . . . . . . .200.00 – 375.00

    Jardiniere and Pedestal, Shape #2881 . . . . . . . . . . . . . . . . . .500.00 – 750.00

    Jardiniere and Pedestal, Shape #2060 . . . . . . . . . . . . . . . . . .600.00 – 800.00

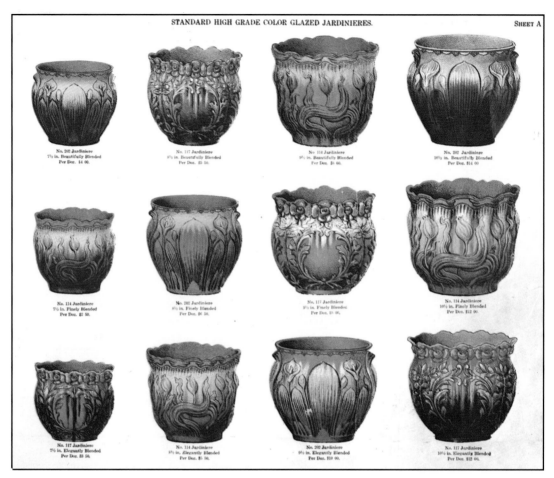

Blended Glaze

Row 1:

    Jardiniere, 7½", Shape #202 . . . . . . . . . . . . . . . . . . . . . . . . . . .$95.00 – 130.00
    Jardiniere, 8½", Shape #117 . . . . . . . . . . . . . . . . . . . . . . . . . . .100.00 – 140.00
    Jardiniere, 9½", Shape #114 . . . . . . . . . . . . . . . . . . . . . . . . . . .125.00 – 150.00
    Jardiniere, 10½", Shape #202 . . . . . . . . . . . . . . . . . . . . . . . . . . .140.00 – 160.00

Row 2:

    Jardiniere, 7½", Shape #114 . . . . . . . . . . . . . . . . . . . . . . . . . . .125.00 – $150.00
    Jardiniere, 8½", Shape #202 . . . . . . . . . . . . . . . . . . . . . . . . . . .100.00 – 140.00
    Jardiniere, 9½", Shape #117 . . . . . . . . . . . . . . . . . . . . . . . . . . .125.00 – 150.00
    Jardiniere, 10½", Shape #114 . . . . . . . . . . . . . . . . . . . . . . . . . . .140.00 – 160.00

Row 3:

    Jardiniere, 7½", Shape #117 . . . . . . . . . . . . . . . . . . . . . . . . . . .95.00 – 130.00
    Jardiniere, 8½", Shape #114 . . . . . . . . . . . . . . . . . . . . . . . . . . .100.00 – 140.00
    Jardiniere, 9½", Shape #202 . . . . . . . . . . . . . . . . . . . . . . . . . . .125.00 – 150.00
    Jardiniere, 10½", Shape #117 . . . . . . . . . . . . . . . . . . . . . . . . . . .140.00 – 160.00

Blended Glaze

Row 1:

      Umbrella Stand, 20", Shape #65 . . . . . . . . . . . . . . . . . . . . . . .$400.00 – 600.00

      Umbrella Stand, 18", Shape #63 . . . . . . . . . . . . . . . . . . . . . . .200.00 – 300.00

      Umbrella Stand, 17", Shape #64 . . . . . . . . . . . . . . . . . . . . . . .185.00 – 250.00

      Umbrella Stand, 21", Shape #72 . . . . . . . . . . . . . . . . . . . . . . .500.00 – 850.00

Row 2:

      Umbrella Stand, 21", Shape #114 . . . . . . . . . . . . . . . . . . . . . . .500.00– 650.00

      Umbrella Stand, 21", Shape #69, . . . . . . . . . . . . . . . . . . . . . . .500.00 – 650.00

      Umbrella Stand, 21", Shape #63 . . . . . . . . . . . . . . . . . . . . . . .450.00 – 600.00

Utility Ware and Cuspidors

Row 1:

 Jugs, Shape #27, 28, &29 . . . . . . . . . . . . . . . . . . . . . . . . . . . . .$50.00 – 125.00

 Four-Pint Jug, Shape #36 . . . . . . . . . . . . . . . . . . . . . . . . . . . . .100.00 – 175.00

 Corn Pitcher, Shape #44 . . . . . . . . . . . . . . . . . . . . . . . . . . . . . .190.00 – 250.00

 Tulip Jug, Shape #25 . . . . . . . . . . . . . . . . . . . . . . . . . . . . . . . . .125.00 – 200.00

 Daisy Jug, Shape #34 . . . . . . . . . . . . . . . . . . . . . . . . . . . . . . . . .125.00 – 200.00

Row 2:

 Four-Pint Jug, Shape #23 . . . . . . . . . . . . . . . . . . . . . . . . . . . . .150.00 – 225.00

 Iris Jug, Shape #43 . . . . . . . . . . . . . . . . . . . . . . . . . . . . . . . . . .150.00 – 225.00

 Holland Jug, Shape #32 . . . . . . . . . . . . . . . . . . . . . . . . . . . . . . .190.00 – 250.00

 Indian Village Jug, Shape #40 . . . . . . . . . . . . . . . . . . . . . . . . . .200.00 – 325.00

 Mug, Shape 41 . . . . . . . . . . . . . . . . . . . . . . . . . . . . . . . . . . . . .100.00 – 175.00

Row 3:

 Old Mill Jug, Shape #31 . . . . . . . . . . . . . . . . . . . . . . . . . . . . . .175.00 – 250.00

 Bristol Glaze Jug, Shape #32 . . . . . . . . . . . . . . . . . . . . . . . . . . .150.00 – 225.00

 Bristol Glaze Jug, Shape #43 . . . . . . . . . . . . . . . . . . . . . . . . . . .150.00 – 225.00

 Cuspidor, Shape #1 . . . . . . . . . . . . . . . . . . . . . . . . . . . . . . . . . .100.00 – 175.00

 Cuspidor, Shape #5 . . . . . . . . . . . . . . . . . . . . . . . . . . . . . . . . . .125.00 – 200.00

Row 4:

 Cuspidor, Shape #4 . . . . . . . . . . . . . . . . . . . . . . . . . . . . . . . . . .95.00 – 150.00

 Cuspidor, Shape #10 . . . . . . . . . . . . . . . . . . . . . . . . . . . . . . . . .115.00 – 175.00

 Cuspidor, Shape #2 . . . . . . . . . . . . . . . . . . . . . . . . . . . . . . . . . .135.00 – 190.00

 Frog Cuspidor, Shape #3 . . . . . . . . . . . . . . . . . . . . . . . . . . . . . .150.00 – 215.00

 Cuspidor, Shape #7 . . . . . . . . . . . . . . . . . . . . . . . . . . . . . . . . . .140.00 – 200.00

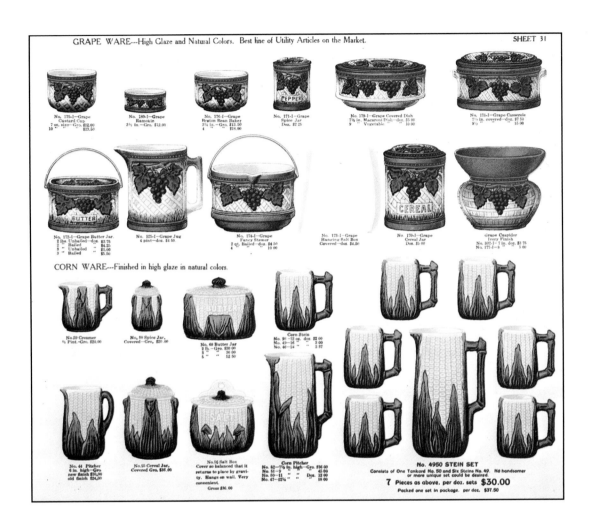

Grape Ware, 1912

Corn Ware, 1912

Row 1:

Grape Custard Cup, Shape #175-1 . . . . . . . . . .$125.00 – 165.00
Grape Ramekin, Shape #180-1 . . . . . . . . . . . . .95.00 – 135.00
Grape Bean Baker, Shape #176-1 . . . . . . . . . . .125.00 – 175.00
Grape Spice Jar, Shape #171-1 . . . . . . . . . . . . .195.00 – 225.00
Grape Covered Dish, Shape #179-1 . . . . . . . . .225.00 – 250.00
Grape Casserole, Shape #178-1 . . . . . . . . . . . .235.00 – 275.00

Row 2:

Grape Butter Jar, Shape #172-1 . . . . . . . . . . . .250.00 – 290.00
Grape Jug, Shape #125-1 . . . . . . . . . . . . . . . . .225.00 – 250.00
Grape Fancy Stewer, Shape #174-1 . . . . . . . . .250.00 – 300.00
Grape Hanging Salt Box, Shape #173-1 . . . . . .350.00 – 450.00
Grape Cereal Jar, Shape #170-1 . . . . . . . . . . . .275.00 – 350.00
Grape Cuspidor, Shape #302-1 & 177-1 . . . . . . .175.00 – 300.00

Row 3:

Corn Creamer, Shape #59 . . . . . . . . . . . . . . . .$175.00 – 225.00
Corn Spice Jar, Shape #58 . . . . . . . . . . . . . . . . .95.00 – 185.00
Corn Butter Jar, Shape #60 . . . . . . . . . . . . . . . .295.00 – 395.00
Corn Steins, Shape #98, 43, 46 . . . . . . . . . . . .$100.00 – 200.00

Row 4:

Corn Pitcher, Shape #44 . . . . . . . . . . . . . . . . . .195.00 – 250.00
Corn Cereal Jar, Shape #55 . . . . . . . . . . . . . . . .285.00 – 375.00
Corn Covered Salt Box, Shape #56 . . . . . . . . . .355.00 – 425.00
Corn Tankards, Shape #52, 51, 50, 47 . . . . . . . .200.00 – 400.00
Corn Stein Set, Shape #4950 . . . . . . . . . . . . . .800.00 – 1,200.00

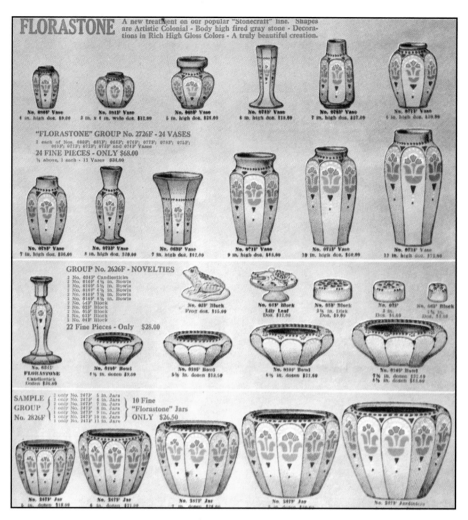

Florastone, 1926

Row 1:

    Vase, 4", Shape #080F . . . . . . . . . . . . . . . . . . . . . . . . . . . . . . .$300.00 – 400.00

    Vase, 3", Shape #081F . . . . . . . . . . . . . . . . . . . . . . . . . . . . . . .250.00 – 350.00

    Vase, 5", Shape #068F . . . . . . . . . . . . . . . . . . . . . . . . . . . . . . .350.00 – 450.00

    Vase, 6", Shape #074F . . . . . . . . . . . . . . . . . . . . . . . . . . . . . . .400.00 – 500.00

    Vase, 7", Shape #076F . . . . . . . . . . . . . . . . . . . . . . . . . . . . . . .450.00 – 550.00

    Vase, 6", Shape #077F . . . . . . . . . . . . . . . . . . . . . . . . . . . . . . .350.00 – 500.00

Row 2:

    Vase, 7", Shape #078F . . . . . . . . . . . . . . . . . . . . . . . . . . . . . . .450.00 – 550.00

    Vase, 8", Shape #075F . . . . . . . . . . . . . . . . . . . . . . . . . . . . . . .500.00 – 600.00

    Vase, 7", Shape #069F . . . . . . . . . . . . . . . . . . . . . . . . . . . . . . .500.00 – 600.00

    Vase, 9", Shape #071F . . . . . . . . . . . . . . . . . . . . . . . . . . . . . . .550.00 – 700.00

    Vase, 10", Shape #072F . . . . . . . . . . . . . . . . . . . . . . . . . . . . . .650.00 – 800.00

    Vase, 12", Shape #073F . . . . . . . . . . . . . . . . . . . . . . . . . . . . . .850.00 – 1,100.00

Row 3:

    Block Frog, Shape #03F . . . . . . . . . . . . . . . . . . . . . . . . . . . . . .400.00 – 600.00

    Block Lily Leaf, Shape #04F . . . . . . . . . . . . . . . . . . . . . . . . . .300.00 – 500.00

    Block, Shape #05F, 3 sizes . . . . . . . . . . . . . . . . . . . . . . . . . . . .100.00 – 225.00

Row 4:

    Candlestick, Shape #034F . . . . . . . . . . . . . . . . . . . . . . . . . . .500.00 – 650.00 pr.

    Flower Bowls, Shape #010F, 4 sizes . . . . . . . . . . . . . . . . . . . .200.00 – 400.00

Row 5:

    Jardiniere, Shape #247F, 5 sizes . . . . . . . . . . . . . . . . . . . . . . .250.00 – 750.00

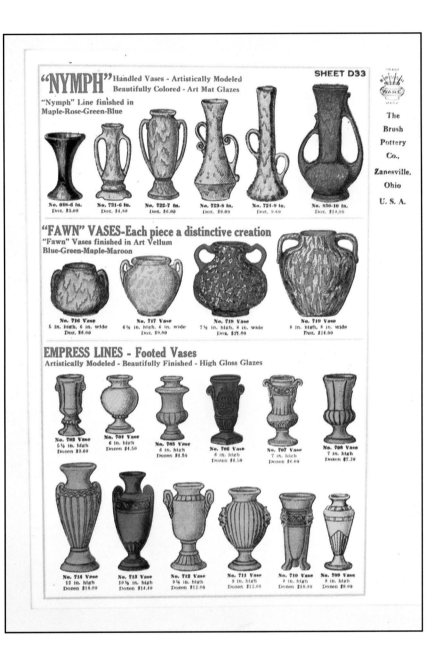

Nymph, 1933

Row 1:
    Vase, 6", Shape #048 . . . . . . . . . .$35.00 – 50.00
    Vase, 6", Shape #721 . . . . . . . . . .40.00 – 60.00
    Vase, 7", Shape #722 . . . . . . . . . .45.00 – 75.00
    Vase, 8", Shape #723 . . . . . . . . . .55.00 – 75.00
    Vase, 9", Shape #724 . . . . . . . . . .65.00 – 85.00
    Vase, 10", Shape #830 . . . . . . . . . .70.00 – 85.00

Fawn, 1933

Row 2:
    Vase, 5", Shape #716 . . . . . . . . . .30.00 – 60.00
    Vase, 6½", Shape #717 . . . . . . . . . .60.00 – 75.00
    Vase, 7½", Shape #718 . . . . . . . . . .70.00 – 85.00
    Vase, 8", Shape #719 . . . . . . . . . .85.00 – 100.00

Empress, 1933

Row 3:
    Vase, 5½", Shape #703 . . . . . . . . . .35.00 – 55.00
    Vase, 6", Shape #704 . . . . . . . . . .35.00 – 55.00
    Vase, 6", Shape #705 . . . . . . . . . .35.00 – 55.00
    Vase, 6", Shape #706 . . . . . . . . . .35.00 – 55.00
    Vase, 7", Shape #707 . . . . . . . . . .35.00 – 55.00
    Vase, 7", Shape #708 . . . . . . . . . .35.00 – 55.00

Row 4:
    Vase, 12", Shape #714 . . . . . . . .120.00 – 150.00
    Vase, 10½", Shape #713 . . . . . . .100.00 – 120.00
    Vase, 9½", Shape #712 . . . . . . .100.00 – 120.00
    Vase, 9", Shape #711 . . . . . . . .140.00 – 160.00
    Vase, 8", Shape #710 . . . . . . . .140.00 – 160.00
    Vase, 8", Shape #709 . . . . . . . .130.00 – 150.00

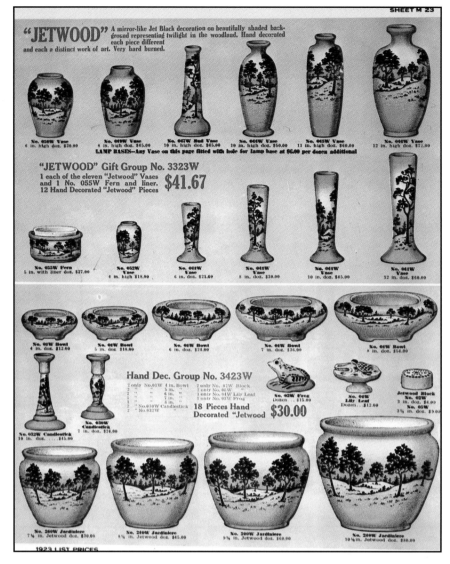

Jetwood, 1923

Row 1:

    Vase, 6", Shape #050W . . . . . . . . . . . . . . . . . . . . . . . . . . . . . .$400.00 – 550.00

    Vase, 8", Shape #049W . . . . . . . . . . . . . . . . . . . . . . . . . . . . . .475.00 – 600.00

    Vase, 10", Shape #047W . . . . . . . . . . . . . . . . . . . . . . . . . . . . .500.00 – 700.00

    Vase, 10", Shape #044W . . . . . . . . . . . . . . . . . . . . . . . . . . . . .750.00 – 950.00

    Vase, 11", Shape #045W . . . . . . . . . . . . . . . . . . . . . . . . . . . . .650.00 – 750.00

    Vase, 12", Shape #046W . . . . . . . . . . . . . . . . . . . . . . . .1,000.00 – 1,300.00

Row 2:

    Fern Dish, 5", Shape #055W . . . . . . . . . . . . . . . . . . . . . . . . .400.00 – 500.00

    Vase, 4", Shape #052W . . . . . . . . . . . . . . . . . . . . . . . . . . . . .300.00 – 400.00

    Vase, 6", Shape #041W, 4 sizes . . . . . . . . . . . . . . . . . . . . . . .250.00 – 700.00

Row 3:

    Flower Bowls, Shape #01W, 5 sizes . . . . . . . . . . . . . . . . . . . .180.00 – 450.00

Row 4:

    Candlestick, Shape #032W . . . . . . . . . . . . . . . . . . . . . . . . . . .400.00 – 500.00

    Candlestick, Shape #030W . . . . . . . . . . . . . . . . . . . . . . . . . . .325.00 – 400.00

    Frog, Shape #03W . . . . . . . . . . . . . . . . . . . . . . . . . . . . . . . . .400.00 – 600.00

    Lily Leaf, Shape #04W . . . . . . . . . . . . . . . . . . . . . . . . . . . . . .350.00 – 550.00

    Block, Shape #02W, 2 sizes . . . . . . . . . . . . . . . . . . . . . . . . . .150.00 – 250.00

Row 5:

    Jardiniere, Shape #240W, 4 sizes . . . . . . . . . . . . . . . . . . . . . .400.00 – 800.00

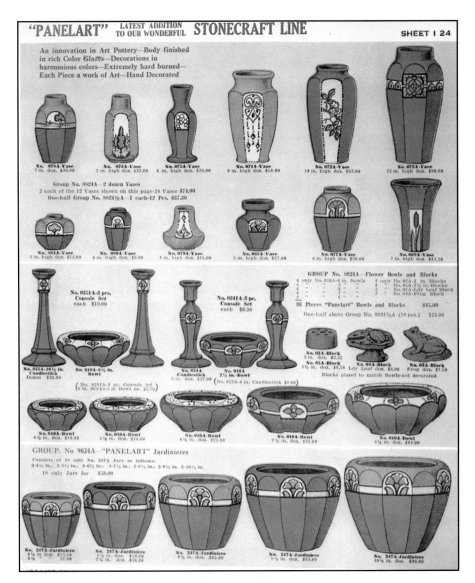

Panelart, 1924

Row 1:

    Vase, 7", Shape #078A . . . . . . . . . . . . . . . . . . .$550.00 – 850.00

    Vase, 7", Shape #076A . . . . . . . . . . . . . . . . . . .500.00 – 800.00

    Vase, 8", Shape #075A . . . . . . . . . . . . . . . . . . .600.00 – 800.00

    Vase, 9", Shape #071A . . . . . . . . . . . . . . .1,000.00 – 1,300.00

    Vase, 10", Shape #072A . . . . . . . . . . . . . . .1,100.00 – 1,400.00

    Vase, 12", Shape #073A . . . . . . . . . . . . . . .1,400.00 – 1,600.00

Row 2:

    Vase, 3", Shape #081A . . . . . . . . . . . . . . . . . . .300.00 – 400.00

    Vase, 4", Shape #080A . . . . . . . . . . . . . . . . . . .350.00 – 450.00

    Vase, 4", Shape #079A . . . . . . . . . . . . . . . . . . .350.00 – 450.00

    Vase, 5", Shape #068A . . . . . . . . . . . . . . . . . . .375.00 – 475.00

    Vase, 6", Shape #077A . . . . . . . . . . . . . . . . . . .450.00 – 600.00

    Vase, 7", Shape #069A . . . . . . . . . . . . . . . . . . .500.00 – 650.00

Row 3:

    Candlestick, Shape #035A . . . . . . . . . . . . . . . . . .400.00 – 550.00

    Candlestick, Shape #034A . . . . . . . . . . . . . . . . . .325.00 – 400.00

    Block, Shape #02A . . . . . . . . . . . . . . . . . . . . . . .150.00 – 250.00

    Block, Shape #04A . . . . . . . . . . . . . . . . . . . . . . .350.00 – 550.00

    Frog Block, Shape #03A . . . . . . . . . . . . . . . . . .400.00 – 550.00

Row 4:

    Flower Bowls, Shape #010A, 5 sizes . . . . . . . . .200.00 – 500.00

Row 5:

    Jardiniere, Shape #247A, 5 sizes . . . . . . . . . . . .450.00 – 900.00

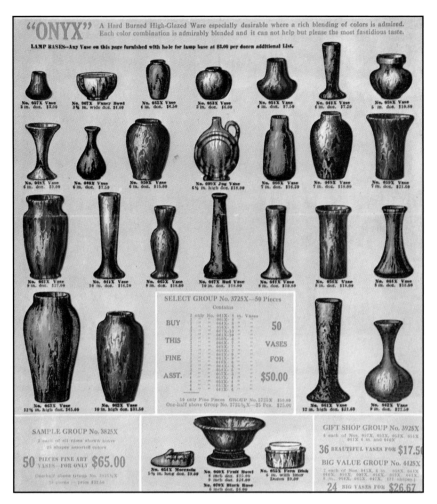

Onyx, 1925

Row 1:

    Vase, 3", Shape #057X . . . . . . . . . . . . . .$35.00 – 65.00

    Fancy Bowl, Shape #067X . . . . . . . . . . .35.00 – 75.00

    Vase, 4", Shape #032X . . . . . . . . . . . .75.00 – 115.00

    Vase, 3", Shape #053X . . . . . . . . . . . . .35.00 – 70.00

    Vase, 4", Shape #051X . . . . . . . . . . . . .40.00 – 80.00

    Vase, 6", Shape #041X . . . . . . . . . . . . .35.00 – 50.00

    Vase, 5", Shape #058X . . . . . . . . . . . . .50.00 – 75.00

Row 2:

    Vase, 6", Shape #048X . . . . . . . . . . . . .50.00 – 75.00

    Vase, 6", Shape #040X . . . . . . . . . . . . .55.00 – 80.00

    Vase, 6", Shape #050X . . . . . . . . . . . . .50.00 – 75.00

    Jug vase, 6½", Shape #099X . . . . . . . . . .50.00 – 75.00

    Vase, 7", Shape #066X . . . . . . . . . . . . .60.00 – 90.00

    Vase, 7", Shape #049X . . . . . . . . . . . . .50.00 – 80.00

    Vase, 7", Shape #059X . . . . . . . . . . . . .70.00 – 95.00

Row 3:

    Vase, 9", Shape #061X . . . . . . . . . . . . .75.00 – 100.00

    Vase, 10", Shape #041X . . . . . . . . . . . .45.00 – 80.00

    Vase, 8", Shape #065X . . . . . . . . . . . .65.00 – 80.00

    Bud vase, 10", Shape #047X . . . . . . . . . .65.00 – 90.00

    Vase, 8", Shape #041X . . . . . . . . . . . . .35.00 – 50.00

    Vase, 8", Shape #056X . . . . . . . . . . . .75.00 – 100.00

    Vase, 8", Shape #064X . . . . . . . . . . . . .60.00 – 100.00

Row 4:

    Vase, 12½", Shape #063X . . . . . . . . . .125.00 – 160.00

    Vase, 10", Shape #041X . . . . . . . . . . . .75.00 – 125.00

    Vase, 12", Shape #041X . . . . . . . . . . . .75.00 – 125.00

    Vase, 9", Shape #042X . . . . . . . . . . . . .80.00 – 130.00

Row 5

    Moccasin, 5½", Shape #054X . . . . . . . .150.00 – 250.00

    Fruit Bowl, Shape #060X, 2 sizes . . . . . .75.00 – 125.00

    Fern Dish, Shape #053X . . . . . . . . . . .100.00 – 150.00

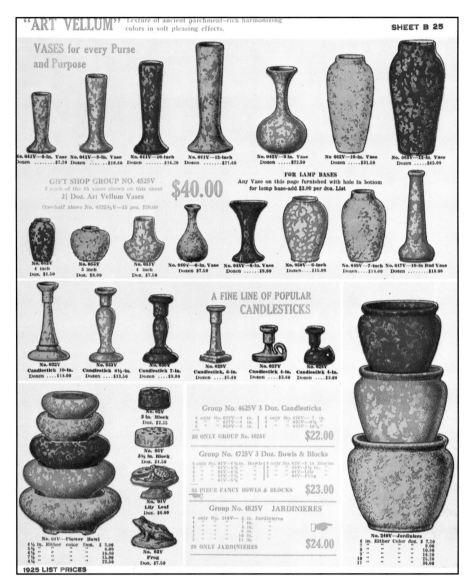

Art Kellum, 1925

Row 1:

    Vase, 6", Shape #041V . . . . . . . . . . . . . . . . . . . . . .$40.00 – 50.00

    Vase, 8", Shape #041V . . . . . . . . . . . . . . . . . . . . .50.00 – 60.00

    Vase, 10", Shape #041V . . . . . . . . . . . . . . . . . . . .60.00 – 75.00

    Vase, 9", Shape #042V . . . . . . . . . . . . . . . . . . .125.00 – 165.00

    Vase, 10", Shape #062V . . . . . . . . . . . . . . . . . . .115.00 – 135.00

    Vase, 12", Shape #063V . . . . . . . . . . . . . . . . . . .135.00 – 175.00

Row 2:

    Vase, 4", Shape #052V . . . . . . . . . . . . . . . . . . . .75.00 – 100.00

    Vase, 3", Shape #053V . . . . . . . . . . . . . . . . . . . .45.00 – 85.00

    Vase, 4", Shape #051V . . . . . . . . . . . . . . . . . . . .60.00 – 90.00

    Vase, 6", Shape #040V . . . . . . . . . . . . . . . . . . . .75.00 – 115.00

    Vase, 6", Shape #048V . . . . . . . . . . . . . . . . . . . .85.00 – 125.00

    Vase, 6", Shape #050V . . . . . . . . . . . . . . . . . . . .40.00 – 55.00

    Vase, 7", Shape #049V . . . . . . . . . . . . . . . . . . . .65.00 – 95.00

    Vase, 10", Shape #047V . . . . . . . . . . . . . . . . . . .100.00 – 125.00

Row 3:

    Candlestick, Shape #032V . . . . . . . . . . . . . . . . .125.00 – 150.00

    Candlestick, Shape #033V . . . . . . . . . . . . . . . . .115.00 – 130.00

    Candlestick, Shape #030V . . . . . . . . . . . . . . . . .100.00 – 125.00

    Candlestick, Shape #029V . . . . . . . . . . . . . . . . .100.00 – 125.00

    Candlestick, Shape #028V . . . . . . . . . . . . . . . . .75.00 – 100.00

    Candlestick, Shape #027V . . . . . . . . . . . . . . . . .75.00 – 100.00

Row 4:

    Flower Bowl, Shape #01V, 5 sizes . . . . . . . . . . . . .55.00 – 135.00

    Flower Frog, Shape #03V . . . . . . . . . . . . . . . . . .125.00 – 150.00

    Lily Leaf, Shape #04V . . . . . . . . . . . . . . . . . . . .125.00 – 150.00

    Flower Block, Shape #05V . . . . . . . . . . . . . . . . . .25.00 – 35.00

    Flower Block, Shape #02V . . . . . . . . . . . . . . . . . .35.00 – 45.00

    Jardiniere, Shape #240V, 6 sizes . . . . . . . . . . . . .135.00 – 350.00

# BIBLIOGRAPHY

Barnett, W. Clare and Lucile (Brush); from their records, memories, private correspondence and conversations.

*The Brush Pottery Company Blue Book*; printed by the Company, 1972

The Brush Pottery Office Files; minute book of the J. W. McCoy, Brush McCoy and Brush Potteries (1905 – 35), photos, legal papers, catalogs of J. W. McCoy, Brush-McCoy and Brush Potteries, payroll book of the first Brush Pottery, insurance papers, card file, letterheads.

*China, Glass and Lamps*, Death Calls Leaders in Allied Trades, March 1934.

*Crockery and Glass Journal*, From Tombstones to Crockery; April 1929

Cusick, Jay; material concerning his father, photo.

Evan, Paul, *Art Pottery of the United States, An Encyclopedia of Producers and Their Marks*; published by Charles Scribner's Sons, N. Y., 1974.

Lewis, Thomas, *History: Zanesville and Muskingum County, Ohio*, published by S. J. Clark Publishing Company, Chicago, Ill., Vol. 1, pgs. 493, 1482, Vol. II, pgs. 555, 623.

Longstreth, Mrs. Helen Jamieson; from her remembrances of the pottery.

McCoy, Mrs. Nelson; copy of J. W. McCoy obituary from Roseville newspapers, Dec. 1914.

Muskingum County Court House, Records of Deeds; from the book of real estate transfers, copied by Att'y John Ringhisen, Deed book 102, pg. 318, Deed book 143, pg. 119.

Radford, Fred, *A Radford Pottery, His Life and Works*, published by the author, 1973.

Report of Asst. Sec. James R. March, State of Ohio, in reference to the standings of these potteries; The Brush Pottery (incorporated 12-10-06, dissolved 1-8-12), J. B. Owens Pottery (9-24-1891 to 4-19-07), Zanesville Tile Co. (10-16-05 to 11-16-36).

Schneider, Norris: *Roseville Grew Rapidly During 1890 Boom*, Sunday Times Signal, Zanesville, Ohio, Aug. 2, 1959; from his article on "The Brighton Area," in Zanesville, Ohio newspaper, 1967; *Zanesville Art Pottery*, published by the author, 1963.

Smith, Wilbur; list of decorators.

Tatman, John; copy of obituary of A. C. Tatman, Zanesville newspaper.

United States Patent Office, Records of application for M-I-T-U-S-A trademark, 11-28-14.

*Zanesville City Directory*, 1907; copied by Norris Schneider, list of the officers of the first Brush Pottery, and pertinent information.

*Zanesville Daily Courier*, Brush-McCoy Pottery Now Ready For Business, Dec. 14, 1911.

# INDEX

# Schroeder's
# ANTIQUES
## Price Guide

. . . is the #1 best-selling antiques & collectibles value guide on the market today, and here's why . . .

**Schroeder's ANTIQUES Price Guide**

*OUR #1 BEST SELLER!*

**Identification & Values Of Over 50,000 Antiques & Collectibles**

*8½ x 11, 608 Pages, $14.95*

• *More than 300 advisors, well-known dealers, and top-notch collectors work together with our editors to bring you accurate information regarding pricing and identification.*

• *More than 45,000 items in almost 500 categories are listed along with hundreds of sharp original photos that illustrate not only the rare and unusual, but the common, popular collectibles as well.*

• *Each large close-up shot shows important details clearly. Every subject is represented with histories and background information, a feature not found in any of our competitors' publications.*

• *Our editors keep abreast of newly developing trends, often adding several new categories a year as the need arises.*

If it merits the interest of today's collector, you'll find it in *Schroeder's*. And you can feel confident that the information we publish is up to date and accurate. Our advisors thoroughly check each category to spot inconsistencies, listings that may not be entirely reflective of market dealings, and lines too vague to be of merit. Only the best of the lot remains for publication.

Without doubt, you'll find
**SCHROEDER'S ANTIQUES PRICE GUIDE**
the only one to buy for
reliable information and values.

**COLLECTOR BOOKS**
*A Division of Schroeder Publishing Co., Inc.*